BREAKING BREAD

Breaking Bread

ROB FROST

KINGSWAY PUBLICATIONS
EASTBOURNE

Printed in Great Britain for
KINGSWAY PUBLICATIONS LTD
Lottbridge Drove, Eastbourne, E. Sussex BN23 6NT by
Cox & Wyman Ltd, Reading.
Typeset by CST, Eastbourne, E. Sussex

Contents

TO
all my mad friends who hammer up and down the
motorways with me as we go to share worship
workshops around the country.
Much of my thinking has been shaped by conversations
over greasy chips in the early hours of the morning!

Thanks to Helen Found and Clive Jones for additional
research, and to Meryl Smith and Helen Hartwell
for typing the final manuscript

INTRODUCTION

The Concept

Breaking Bread is a musical setting of the Holy Communion service, but more than that it's a project to encourage new initiatives in worship. This book accompanies the album, songbook and service book. It is designed to stimulate fresh ideas and attitudes among those who sit in the pew, as well as those who regularly lead worship.

The workshop sessions at the end of each chapter are designed for use in house groups, youth fellowships, 'Consultations on Worship' and church conferences. They are a basis for discussion and action about worship. The activities have been tried out in group work, but please feel free to amend or adapt anything to suit your own situation.

Please be assured that none of the material contained is written out of malice or contempt. I send this book out with the prayer that it may be a means of inspiring many people to make worship really meaningful. Worship need never be a bore!

The Garden Tomb

I stood in quiet reverence. I had reached the destination of my pilgrimage. The long hours of travel and the many weeks of preparation were behind me. I was standing beside the Garden Tomb in Jerusalem.

This spot had become the focal point of my travels, the place where I would pause to remember the events of that first Easter morning. 'Come,' said the elderly guide, 'step inside and see—the tomb is empty.'

I stepped into the cave and turned to look out to the beautiful garden beyond. In my mind, I re-ran the events of Easter morning. I saw Mary Magdalene approaching the tomb with the spices in her hand, I saw her surprise at finding the body gone. I heard her cry of despair to the gardener: 'They have taken my Lord away, and I do not know where they have put him!'

But this was no gardener, this was the risen Lord. Christ had overcome the power of death and opened the way to eternal life. Christ had risen triumphant over the power of evil, and anticipated the final victory. Christ had defeated the power of suffering, and risen victorious to be our source of renewing strength.. Christ had risen from the dead . . . the celebration could begin!

The Resurrection is the seal of the New Covenant, the assurance that Christ has won the victory. This is the very heart of our faith. 'And if Christ has not been raised,' wrote Paul, 'then your faith is a delusion and you are still lost in your sins' (1 Cor 15:17).

There in that dark tomb, overcome by emotion, I paused and reflected. I was standing at the birthplace of Christian worship. I had traced the celebration to its source. Christian worship was born in a tomb.

We meet in an unbroken tradition that stems from that wonderful Easter morning. We come to celebrate the risen Christ. We come because he promised, 'Where two or three are gathered together in my name, there am I in the midst of them.'

I

A New Thing

The driver clambered aboard the huge yellow crane. The engine roared. A black cloud of choking exhaust bellowed from the pipe above the cab.

The moment had arrived, and I will never forget it. As the tiny group of church members stood silently and watched, the gantry moved gently to and fro. A huge ball suspended from the crane began to swing. There was an echoing crunch as it slammed into the masonry. Again and again the gantry swung and the ball cracked the brickwork. The engine roared again. This time the ball plunged through the chapel wall. Bricks crashed down in clusters and plaster fell like a mist. The woodwork inside splintered and snapped.

The chapel was coming down. Generations had worshipped in this place, and I was the minister to watch its demolition. I was deeply moved. I thought of countless people who had met within those walls to sing their praises, plead their prayers, mourn their dead and bless their new born. It was the end of an era.

Deep in the ruins, the demolition gang came across a glass bottle buried beneath the foundation stone. A greeting of Christian love from the church leaders who had built the chapel nearly a century before; people of vision, of dedication and of faith. I wondered what those church leaders of long ago would have made of it all. Their chapel, for which they'd worked so hard, was razed to the ground.

I hoped they would understand, for this demolition was not a sign of defeat but a sign that the church of Christ was moving on. The demolition of that building opened the way for a new direction in worship and a new dimension of faith, for that small congregation. It did not mean the death of the church in that area; it was the symbol of a new beginning. The new multi-purpose worship centre was far more relevant to the needs of the emerging church than the rigid lay-out of the previous sanctuary.

That's what the history of the church is all about! New beginnings! All through history Christ's church has been moving on, despite those who try to stand in its way. Our Sunday worship is part of an ongoing tradition which has crossed many centuries.

Worship is a living form. Nothing in the Bible says that services should be constructed in one set way. Nowhere is it carved in stone that they must contain five hymns, two readings, three prayers and a sermon. I'm amused when people say that some forms of worship aren't 'traditional'. I'm tempted to ask them: Which of the church's many traditions are they appealing to as the 'norm'?

Are they appealing to the Jewish tradition of worship, which so influenced the development of Christianity? In the years after the Exile there was a growing desire to worship at home. Ceremonies and prayers within the life of the family were seen as very important in that tradition.

Or are they thinking of the early church tradition, when Christians met daily in the Temple, shared meals in each other's homes and lived in eager anticipation of Christ's imminent return?

Perhaps they're thinking of the great fathers of the early church such as Justin Martyr, Tertullian and Cyprian—who each founded different strands of liturgical tradition.

Or do they look to the tradition of the church after the conversion of Constantine? Suddenly the church wasn't a persecuted minority, but a religion, recognized by the State. The homely services disappeared and large churches dependent on clerical leadership grew popular. Gradually those in the East began to look towards Jerusalem and Antioch for their tradition, whereas those in the West looked to Rome.

Is the 'right' tradition that which developed during the Middle Ages? The services were read by clergy, while the congregation sat and watched like silent spectators.

Or are they looking to the Reformation as the correct tradition to follow? The Reformers tried to communicate in the language of the people, to restore preaching to central prominence and to discard set prayers.

Each century has brought many new 'traditions'. For example: the major liturgical reforms under Thomas Cranmer in the seventeenth century; the great musical tradition of the Wesleys in the eighteenth century; the liturgy of the Oxford Movement in the nineteenth century; and the major influence of Vatican II on worship in the twentieth century.

If we are to be true to the 'tradition' of church worship, we need to understand how rich and diverse that tradition is! I recently sat in the midday mass in St Mark's Basilica in Venice and watched the priests celebrate the 'Feast'. I couldn't understand a word of what was being said, but it was good to be in the house of God and to sense his presence. Nothing could be further from the tradition of the mission hall in which I was reared. Yet God was there, and I sensed a mystic unity with Christians down all the centuries.

As the mass continued, I looked up at the golden mosaics glinting in the sunlight and gazed at the figure of Christ on the cross. This picture is ten centuries old but it still speaks today. As I sat in worship I was deeply aware of the great tradition of worship which we all share.

A church without a sense of the past has no roots, but if it is locked in the past it has no future. A church can't live on tradition, but neither can it live properly without a sense of its rich heritage. It must allow the past to enrich, but not to dominate.

A commission of the World Council of Churches met in Crete in 1978 to discuss worship. It declared: 'Faithfulness to tradition requires therefore the utmost sensitivity—to the claims of God who does not change and to the needs of men and women who are always changing.' The church's task is to take hold of the past with one hand and the future with the other, and to shape its worship within this creative tension.

Wherever I travel around Britain I discover groups of Christians who are disillusioned with worship. They are bored with the staleness of services and confess that worship doesn't work. These aren't just young people. Often they are folk in their fifties or sixties. Some of them have given a lifetime of service to the church, but frankly admit that worship is a disappointment.

They work toward the renewal of worship in their local situation but often meet a wall of hostility to any kind of change. In some cases they are working in churches which are bound by traditionalism. They find that worship is trapped in time and cocooned against renewal. Everyone seems to think that the hymn/prayer sandwich is sacrosanct, and that anything else is suspect.

Others are working in churches which are dependent on the clergy. Worship remains a spectator activity. The minister does everything while the congregation looks on. Often such churches are led by those who fear that changes will divide. They guard the status quo, only to discover that tradition can sometimes divide even more deeply.

They may be serving in churches which are frozen by doubt. Faith has burnt low and worship has grown stale. Services are a mourning of faith once held, not a celebration of what God is doing today. The funereal atmosphere harks back to happy days long ago, and there is no joyous anticipation of what is yet to be. The church has become the home of powerless prayer, pointless tradition and sad songs.

Yet in some places God is doing a new thing. Congregations are finding new songs to sing, new prayers to pray and new praises to offer. They follow a living Lord who is alive and active—a God who is moving on. Across all the denominations and throughout all the land there are churches which are discovering a freshness in their worship. New traditions are emerging which are exciting and different.

I believe that these last decades of the twentieth century will one day be seen as a turning point for the renewal of worship. What God is doing is no fringe movement in the backwater of church life. It is the start of something that will affect worship for generations to come. These are exciting days and God is calling us to become part of the church's new and living tradition. We close our doors to this movement at our peril.

Worship as sacrifice

Much of our contemporary worship seems dry and life-less because many of us have lost the art of worship. Worship should take us beyond the sphere of our knowledge and beyond the material universe, to approach One who is superior, pre-eminent, matchless and incomparable.

Adding an extra chorus, using guitars instead of church organs or incorporating drama into services are side issues. Our most urgent task is to learn how to worship as mortal people approaching Immortal God.

We live in an age when man seems to be the focus of everything. He is the tamer of the elements, explorer of the universe, lord of all knowledge and controller of his own destiny. In many circles any talk of the supernatural is taboo. Our plastic hi-tech society is basically materialistic, and there is a dearth of understanding about spiritual things.

The prevalent agnosticism of society has tainted us all. Many of us are incapable of approaching the Almighty; we want services to be 'entertaining', 'enjoyable' and 'inspiring'. We've missed the point of what worship is.

Worship is not primarily for us, it's for God! It is the opportunity for busy people to touch the eternal, for sinners to glimpse the holy, for broken people to be enfolded in perfect Love. Worship is moving beyond our self-centred lives to meet the One who created us for something better.

If a church really does want to renew its worship life, it must first realize that worship demands sacrifice of time, energy, and creativity. The church's highest calling is to be a worshipping community, and it needs to put study, prayer and preparation into its worship life.

> Come, let us bow down and worship him; let us kneel before
> the Lord, our Maker! He is our God; we are the people he
> cares for, the flock for which he provides (Ps 95:6–7).

Too many churches have come to think of worship as an
activity that occurs on Sundays. The Bible teaches, however, that the whole of life is worship. There is no segre-
gation between sacred and secular, between Sunday and
the rest of life. All that we are, all that we do, and all
that we have is to be offered to the One who created us.
Paul wrote:

> So then, my brothers, because of God's great mercy to us I
> appeal to you: Offer yourselves as a living sacrifice to God,
> dedicated to his service and pleasing to him. This is the true
> worship that you should offer (Rom 12:1).

This vivid picture of life as a 'living sacrifice' was a stark
image for Paul's Jewish readers, who thought of sacri-
fices as dead animals offered on altars. But Paul taught
them that the whole of life was to be a sacrifice for the
glory of God. Worship must become a 'living sacrifice'
for us, too.

Worship is about shopping in the supermarket and
driving on congested roads. It's about family relationships and caring for awkward colleagues. It's the frustra-
tion of difficult work, and the joy of a job well done. It's
celebrating the presence of God in the nitty-gritty of
everyday routine. Worship is life itself! 'Everything you
do or say, then,' wrote Paul, 'should be done in the name
of the Lord Jesus, as you give thanks through him to
God the Father' (Col 3:17).

A life which reflects the presence of the Lord is a life
of worship. It's a personality stamped with the transcen-
dent. It's living a daily relationship with Jesus Christ, the

Son of God. When we come to church on Sundays and complain about the minister, the organist or the liturgy —we should think again! For the quality of worship is affected by our way of life and what each of us has to offer.

Worship is what people bring to church, not what they come to receive. When people complain 'I didn't get much out of that service,' I'm tempted to ask, 'But what did you take in to it?' Worship is the offering of our lives to God—not an opportunity to sit back and take in!

Worship is mystery

Worship is also the corporate expression of a local church. Mind you, in some churches you'd be hard pressed to believe it! I've sometimes looked down from the pulpit to see the congregation scattered throughout the sanctuary. One or two are in the gallery, a handful are in one corner and others are sitting apart in the pews. Is this really corporate worship?

I am convinced that a congregation's communal life really affects the quality of its worship. Some congregations never meet except in church on Sundays, and then it isn't a meeting of minds and hearts. A curt 'Good morning' and a limp handshake does not qualify as 'fellowship'.

Where a church gathers together for social events, friendships will form. Where people gather in small groups for discussion and study, relationships will deepen. Where people visit one another in their homes, there will grow a sense of belonging.

I am sure that churches which put time and effort into deepening the sense of community among their people reap dividends in lively worship. But where people sit apart like strangers, the worship stagnates and becomes a cold ritual.

> He is the one who holds the whole building together and makes it grow into a sacred temple dedicated to the Lord. In union with him you too are being built together with all the others into a place where God lives through his Spirit (Eph 2:21–22).

This is the mystery of worship—a congregation must become a 'living temple' bound together by the love of God. There may be people at church with whom we don't get on—but we come as one. It's impossible for a divided congregation to worship with integrity. We live in an age in which people like neat answers. Many like truth to be sold in easily understandable units. Even services are sometimes presented in easy-to-enjoy packages. But worship is essentially a mystery.

As we lift high the name of Jesus Christ in worship, we should be drawn to the everlasting Father. As we approach the One who came for us, died for us and rose again for us, we should glimpse the eternal God. Some of my most precious moments in worship have been opportunities to move beyond the words and to meet the living Lord. This is indeed a wonderful mystery.

> Christ is the visible likeness of the invisible God. He is the first-born Son, superior to all created things. For through him God created everything in heaven and on earth, the seen and the unseen things, including spiritual powers, lords, rulers and authorities. God created the whole universe through him and for him (Col 1:15-16).

But there are other mysteries about worship. There is a sense in which worship mysteriously binds us to the church around the world. As we worship we are part of the great hymn of praise which stretches from continent to continent and from shore to shore.

When I was on mission in Kenya I was invited to stay

in a mud-hut village deep in the bush. As I lay on the straw bed, I listened to dozens of village Christians singing and praising God. Their joy was inspiring and I thanked God for them.

As I looked out through the open door I saw the moon and stars above. I thought of my friends back in Birmingham who were also singing their praises to the Lord that Sunday. My mind raced around the globe and I pictured the great choir of God's people in every continent, united in the praise of God.

I once knew a church organist who really loved the Lord. Shortly before she died she visited Fountains Abbey. It was late evening and it had been a glorious day. As she lingered there alone, she was suddenly overwhelmed by a vision of the heavenly choir—the communion of saints. That experience was a great strength to her in the weeks before she died. It was also a real comfort to those of us who knew her. After she died, when ever I looked down at the empty organ console I remembered her glimpse of the church triumphant!

Whenever we gather for worship we are part of the heavenly choir. The great crowd of witnesses watches from the grandstand of faith. Worship is our highest calling and one day, when we become part of that great host, it will be a mystery no more.

WORKSHOP SESSION ONE

Starter

Join the celebration!

Ask each member of the group to bring photographs of 'celebrations' they have attended: e.g. weddings, birthdays, banquets, social events.

Each person describes the event which is portrayed. The group then discusses: 'What makes a good celebration?'

Ask yourselves: Do we look forward to worship on Sundays?

Is worship really like a 'celebration'?

Should worship be a joyful experience?

How can worship become more like a celebration?

Activity

First trip to church

In groups of three, imagine what it must be like when someone goes to a worship service for the very first time. Everything seems very strange, and they don't know what they are expected to do or to say!

Your group of three is to imagine that you have just got home after your 'first trip to church'. Talk together about your impressions.

Discuss: The building

The people you met

The form of service

The language used

The sermon

The music

The welcome

Use your imagination to make the conversation as hilarious as possible! Role-play several of the conversations in front of the whole group.

Discuss: Would people think they had come to a 'celebration' if they visited your church?

How can our worship be enriched?

Question raiser

The Jews had many prayers, symbols and reminders of their faith in their everyday life. But there often seems a great divide between the 'sacred' and the 'secular' in our contemporary society.

In groups of three, suggest different situations when prayers may be said, phrases read, or symbols displayed to remind us that the whole of life is for the glory of God.

After you have made a list of these situations, create prayers, phrases and symbols which would suit each.

Each group of three then shares its work with the rest.

e.g. Travel:
A prayer before a long journey.
A phrase to be displayed on a car dashboard.
A symbol for the bumper of a Christian driver.

Study:
A prayer at the start of term.
A phrase to be written on your college file.
A symbol for the door of Christian students.

Discuss: How can we learn to make the whole of our lives a 'living sacrifice' to God?
Have services become too 'religious'?
Are they too separate from normal life?

Discussion questions

Divide into groups of three.

Group one: Reads Acts 2:43–47.
Group two: Reads Acts 4:23–31.
Group three: Reads Acts 4:32–37.

Group four: Reads Acts 6:1–7.
Group five: Reads Acts 9:17–25.
Each group must ask: What were the characteristics of the early church?

What would it be like to be a member of such a church?

How does our church compare with the early church?

What can we learn corporately from the life of the early church?

Does the community life of a church affect its worship?

Closing prayers

This section should only last six minutes in total.
1. Read some of the prayers which were written for the Question Raiser section if they seem appropriate.
2. Hand out to the group different missionary magazines, prayer letters, and articles about the church around the world.
   Ask people within the group to read excerpts from these, and then invite individuals to offer prayers of thanksgiving or of intercession for these churches.
3. Talk together about different Christians who have influenced your life, but who have now passed on to join the church 'militant and triumphant'.
   Close by asking one member of the group to thank God that we belong to the church eternal!

2

Learning to Praise

A young minister from the United States came to stay at our church one summer. He brought with him a lively youth group who called themselves 'The King's Kids'. They were great fun to be with, and had a joyous faith in Jesus which they were anxious to share.

Every morning I joined the young minister and 'The King's Kids' for their devotional session in the local park. Their singing, praise and worship was a real inspiration to me; and everyone who came into contact with them seemed to get caught up in this spirit of praise.

I invited them to lead worship one Sunday morning, and they were most thrilled to participate. They prepared a number of beautiful songs and testimonies to share during the worship, and really prayed that the Lord would bless the service.

For over thirty minutes the minister and his youth group conducted a number of songs and praise choruses. Our traditional South London congregation was rather surprised by the easy-going style and the prolonged bout of 'community hymn singing'.

The minister explained to the congregation that they needed time to prepare and that at his church in California they spent forty minutes in song before they felt ready for worship. This was all very well, but some of the congregation were rather annoyed when the service went on until 12.45 p.m.!

As I reflected on the visit of 'The King's Kids' and on the really joyous service we'd shared together, I concluded that the young minister was right. We don't spend long enough in getting ready for worship. More often than not, people rush into church barely a minute before the service, and their minds are not really tuned in to worship. We haven't allowed space for worship and praise to develop at its own pace.

I'm sure that we need to learn how to approach worship, how to prepare for it, how to 'get ready for praise.' If our heart isn't right our worship won't be right—no matter how poetic the liturgy, how popular the preacher or how good our worship songs!

Too many people are allowing their 'feelings' to dictate their attitude to worship. Time and again I've heard people say that they 'didn't feel like worship' last Sunday. This is all wrong! Our worship should not depend on the transient ebb and flow of our emotions, it should be a part of our discipline and discipleship.

The ancient community of Qumran (where the Dead Sea Scrolls were discovered) made it clear that worship was not something that rests on our changes of mood. Manual 10 in the Qumran *Rule of Discipline* says: 'As long as I live it shall be a rule engraved on my tongue, to bring praise like a fruit for an offering and my lips as a sacrificial gift.'

Time and again, the writers of the Psalms urged their readers to make praise a way of life. King David wrote 'I will bless the Lord at all times: his praise shall continually be in my mouth' (Ps 34:1AV). In Psalm 113 we read 'From the rising of the sun unto the going down of the same the Lord's name is to be praised' (Ps 113:3AV), and in Psalm 22, 'O thou that inhabitest the praises of Israel' (Ps 22:3AV).

Praise is an attitude of heart and mind which should be present with us every day of every week. Our service of worship on Sunday should be a culmination of a week of praise to the heavenly Father. We have not come to church to 'sing some hymns' or 'hear a message', we've come first and foremost to express praise to the living God! This spirit of praise should come with the congregation each week. It is not something 'whipped up' by the worship leader or contrived by the minister. It is something offered freely and willingly by the people of God, who have gathered for this express purpose.

Attempts to stir up this kind of praise really leave me cold. One of the few occasions when I have actually walked out of a service was when there was tambourine bashing, hallelujah shouting, hand-clapping emotionalism without any depth. It lacked integrity, sensitivity and a true spirit of reverence, and it proved a distraction from true worship.

The words of Psalm 138 make it plain: 'I will praise thee with my whole heart' (Ps 138:1AV). Praise demands energy, commitment and effort on the part of the whole congregation! It is not sitting back to receive a blessing, it is something given to God from hearts filled with praise. Yet if the truth were really known, most worshippers don't come to church with this attitude. In our heart of hearts many of us would have to admit that we've come with no intention of giving anything. We expect worship to be handed to us on a plate.

Sadly, many of us also come with grudges and grumbles against others. Jesus made it clear that if there were wrong attitudes in our hearts our worship wouldn't be effective. He instructed his disciples to put things right before approaching the altar:

> So if you are about to offer your gift to God at the altar and there you remember that your brother has something against you, leave your gift there in front of the altar, go at once and make peace with your brother, and then come back and offer your gift to God (Mt 5:23).

The Old Testament prophets were equally strict about the need to have right attitudes before participating in worship. The prophet Amos declared: 'Stop your noisy songs; I do not want to listen to your harps. Instead, let justice flow like a stream, and righteousness like a river that never goes dry' (Amos 5:23–24).

It is little wonder that worship is dead and dry if many of us are rolling up to church on Sundays with a bundle of wrong attitudes filling our minds. Many of us have come to criticize the preacher, complain about the hymns or stare into space while angry thoughts fill our hearts.

The fact that we've had a hard week is no excuse either. We may come to church with tears of bereavement in our eyes, or the pain of suffering in our bodies, or a great weight of worry filling our minds. Yet we should still come to bring our burdens to the feet of the Lord and praise him for his willingness to carry them.

Just because our earthly situation has changed—the living God has not! He is as worthy of praise today as he was last week, last month, or last year. It is as we discipline ourselves to sing his praises and glorify his holy name that the worship lifts us to catch a glimpse of paradise. We see beyond the horizon of our human suffering to the greatness of the love of God.

It is when a congregation is prepared for praise, even before they arrive at church, that worship takes off. It's when a congregation is so enthusiastic that they gather early to pray about the worship that things change! It's when people are in tune with God at the start of the worship that the right atmosphere is found.

When a whole congregation catches a glimpse of what a joy 'praising the Lord' can be, the worship takes on a whole new quality. For when the people of Jesus are gathered in his name we have an awesome privilege and responsibility: to share the very best our hearts have to offer!

The meaning of praise

In Hebrew there are many words for 'praise'. The more that you study them, the more you realize how rich Jewish praise has been. As I have reflected on them I have become aware of our need to rediscover what praise can be.

When the Israelites won a great victory over the Canaanite King Jabin, they really praised God. They were led in praise by Deborah and Barak. The word for praise was the word *barak*—so the leader of the worship was someone called 'Praise'!

As Deborah and Barak sang 'Praise the Lord', they were standing in awe of a great God who had given them a wonderful and unexpected victory. The word for praise, *barak*, meant 'to kneel, to kneel down, to salute or to congratulate'. For many free-churchmen like myself it is not easy to kneel down in worship. Kneeling has strong associations with set liturgies and rather musty 'kneelers' in cold stone churches. I've had to 'unlearn' some of my prejudices with regard to kneeling.

When I was present in Bath Cathedral for afternoon

evensong, I really sensed the presence of God. As the April sunshine streamed in through the stained glass windows and the beautiful harmony of the choir filled the air, I found myself kneeling. It wasn't just to 'fit in' with the Anglican custom—it was a genuine expression of an inner attitude at that moment in time. As I knelt in awe of the living God, my heart was bowed before him, and I was humbled by the great sense of his majesty and glory. To kneel before God seemed the most natural thing to do!

Sadly, some of the 'livelier' churches rarely give space for this kind of worship. There is such a strong desire to sing, participate, and make a 'joyful noise' that the moments of quiet wonder get squeezed out. It's hard to find moments for quiet awe and wonder when there is a clamour of voices saying 'Can we sing my favourite chorus?'

We need to master the discipline of the mystics, who were able to kneel before God and wait until they sensed his presence among them. We need to create space for silence, reflection, meditation and peace; moments when we can kneel before the Almighty and glimpse his greatness.

There are numerous references in the Old Testament to the Hebrew word *halal*, which also means praise. The kind of meaning behind this word includes 'to rage, to act foolishly, to boast, to celebrate, or to act madly'. But nothing could be further from the experience of most congregations that I have served over the years. There has been a cool, balanced, orderly atmosphere about many of them!

When the congregation in the vast new Temple of King Solomon worshipped God, they sang 'Praise the Lord, because he is good, and his love is eternal' (Cf. 2 Chron 5:11–14). Here the word for praise is the word *halal*. It was the right kind of word to express what was going on! There were Levites with their cymbals and harps, and 120 priests playing trumpets. The singers were accompanied in perfect harmony by many different kinds of instruments. It was quite a celebration. People were praising God in a very noisy and joyous way—after all, the opening of the Temple was the climax of countless years of work and expectation! As the people praised God in this deafening roar of joy, the cloud of God's presence dazzled them and the presence of the Lord filled the Temple.

I have rarely seen this kind of worship in contemporary services. As we depicted this scene in our musical called 'Visions' at the National Exhibition Centre we had great fun attempting to rediscover what that kind of worship really feels like. The scene was presented by young Anglicans, and I wondered whether any of them had ever worshipped like that before.

On my Sunday evenings off when I lived in Deptford I used to attend worship at the New Testament Church of God. I was often the only white person present in a predominantly West Indian group. There were electric guitars, drums, loud songs and shouts of praise. People frequently danced up and down the aisles and the noise level was closely akin to that of a disco. Yet I often met the living God on those Sunday evenings; I frequently felt that the infectious praise had the anointing of God's power upon it. This was genuine praise, and I wish that many of us who come from different cultural backgrounds could learn to let go of our reserve and join this kind of 'celebration'. It doesn't come easily for me to rage, act foolishly, or act madly in the normal run of church worship—yet I remain convinced that this is part of true worship experience.

There should be services, or space within services,

which really allow people to make a noise—and to 'Let go and let God have his wonderful way'! This will demand a great deal of sensitive teaching and preparation, and the learning of a freedom in our expression which is alien to many of us.

There are also many references to the Hebrew word *zamar*—which also means 'praise'. This word means 'to sing forth, to sing praises or to sing psalms'. Some of the uses of this wonderful word include:

> I will praise him as long as I live;
> I will sing to my God all my life (Ps 146:2).

> Sing praise to God; sing praise to our king!
> God is king over all the world; praise him with song! (Ps 47;6–7).

> Sing for joy to the Lord, all the earth;
> Praise him with songs and shouts of joy! (Ps 98:4).

Congregational singing varies greatly from place to place. One of the most dreadful examples is often found at church weddings. The church organist and I have often sung a duet of 'Love divine all loves excelling', while a congregation of more than a hundred moved their mouths in silence.

Sadly, some church congregations have also adopted this silent approach to singing. Barely a murmur is heard above the sound of the organ and one is left with the impression that the congregation is just 'going through the motions'. This is not *zamar*, it is not genuine praise in song.

I have shared in dozens of workshops for music groups around the country, and have discovered a real lack of understanding about 'sung praise'. I am no musician, but I can tell the difference between those who are making music and those who are 'singing forth praise'. What grieves me about so many musically proficient choirs is that they have not always discovered the spiritual ministry of song. Unless we are tuned in to the leading of the Holy Spirit and our emotions are harnessed in song, church music can be as dry as dust!

Much the same applies to congregations. There is a kind of reverent awe of the hymn book. We sing the words as though they were penned by some scholar locked in cloistered isolation. The fact is that many of our hymns were penned in the heat of suffering, tribulation or temptation. We need to enter into the meaning of the words and make them our own!

As we begin to die to our prejudices in church music and make the words and melodies our own, singing becomes *zamar* in style. As we invest energy, emotion and commitment in our singing, we discover that music can carry us to the throne of God.

As I read the great stories of the eighteenth-century revival and the way that Methodism was 'born in song', I find it interesting that many of the great hymns of Charles Wesley had in excess of eighteen verses. When I have plucked up courage to ask a congregation to sing them in full, I have discovered something strange about the chemistry of long hymns. It takes a congregation four or five verses to 'relax' into a tune and to focus on the meaning of the words. By the twelfth verse they are enjoying *zamar* praise, and by the eighteenth they are breathless and exhausted—but usually quite exhilarated! Surely this is what the charismatic churches have rediscovered in singing simple refrains repeatedly. The congregation has the time to learn the tune, understand the words and make the praise its own.

It has been my privilege to lead the worship at several large Conventions in recent years. The congregations are so enthusiastic, and they want to sing so loud and so long, that it's hard to stop them! The order of service goes out of the window; songs which should take five minutes take fifteen. At times like this I remember that as the Lord inhabited the praises of Israel, he is present in the praises of his people today. Who am I to say 'enough's enough'?

An anthem of the most traditional kind, a hymn of great poetic beauty and theological depth, a great 'Sankey' toe-tapping melody, or a contemporary three-lined chorus—they can all be the opportunity for *zamar* praise. We must take hold of church music and invest the necessary spiritual energy in it to make it really work. Saint Paul summed it up when he wrote to the Colossians: 'Sing hymns and psalms to the Lord with praise in your hearts' (cf. Col 3:16f.).

A growing number of worshippers are starting to raise their arms in worship. Many of those who object to this practice have never asked the question 'Why?' Sadly some of those who raise their arms in worship don't know 'Why' either! For some it's a secret membership signal which says 'I'm a fully paid up charismatic!'

When I was speaking at a Pentecostal ministers' gathering a few months ago I heard one comic suggest that they should organize the refreshments by saying 'Hands down for coffee!' *Buzz* magazine placed an advertisement in its 'small ads' section, inviting readers to write in for 'charismatic arm rests'. These would enable worshippers to keep their hands in the air for much longer periods. Apparently there was a good response to the advertisement, and some people were genuinely surprised to discover that it was an April Fool joke.

There is, however, biblical precedent for raising the arms in worship. The word *yadah* which appears in many of the Psalms means 'To stretch out the hand, confess praise and give thanks'. For example 'All the kings in the world will praise you, Lord, because they have heard your promises' (Ps 138:4).

The beautiful image of the great rulers of the earth 'stretching out their hands' to the King of kings is a good illustration of what *yadah* praise is all about. Another verse reads: 'Praise the Lord! With all my heart I will thank the Lord in the assembly of his people. How wonderful are the things the Lord does!' (Ps 111:1–2).

The raising of arms should be an outward expression of our confidence and trust in the Lord of lords. As we raise our arms we are making a visible demonstration of the awe which fills our hearts. One of the Hebrew words for hand is *yad*, and it is not surprising that the word for praise, *yadah*, is closely associated with raising the hands.

Paul wrote many instructions about worship to Timothy. One of them reads: 'In every church service I want the men to pray, men who are dedicated to God and can lift up their hands in prayer without anger or argument' (1 Tim 2:8).

Personally, I am not a 'good mover'. I move awkwardly. Over the years my team has taught me that movement need not be choreographed, precise or practised. *Yadah* praise suggests that movement is just a way of demonstrating outwardly what we feel inside. Movement during praise has unlocked a new channel of devotion for me. If I can forget others around me I can use movement as a means of communication with the Lord. I am saying with my body what I am feeling with my heart. It is not intended as a means of communication with others, it is just for God.

Having said this, I would rather restrain myself from moving in worship than offend someone else nearby. If my outward expression hinders someone else's worship it's probably doing more harm than good!

The Hebrew word *shabach* means 'to glorify, to give praise', and it appears in Psalm 63: 'Let me see you in the sanctuary; let me see how mighty and glorious you are. Your constant love is better than life itself, and so I will praise you' (Ps 63:2–3).

Perhaps our greatest desire should be to see the glory of the Lord in worship. Moses asked to see the dazzling light of the Lord's presence, and next day on Mount Sinai the Lord came down to him. That was also Isaiah's experience:

> In the year that King Uzziah died, I saw the Lord. He was sitting on his throne, high and exalted, and his robe filled the whole Temple. Round him flaming creatures were standing . . . they were calling out to each other: 'Holy, holy, holy! The Lord Almighty is holy! His glory fills the world' (Is 6:1–3).

Peter, John and James also glimpsed the glory of the Most High. On the Mount of Transfiguration they saw Moses and Elijah talking to Jesus and they glimpsed Christ's glory.

When I was a student at Cliff College Bible School, I remember prayer meetings with the very elderly evangelist Herbert Silverwood, known as the 'firebrand'. As we prayed, he would sometimes cry 'Glory, glory, glory'. I found it quite offputting at first! But soon I realized that this was a tradition which went back for generations. It symbolized a glimpse of the 'glory' of the Lord in worship.

As we come to meet the living God and to know his presence with us, we discover his 'glory'. It is an experience of worship which defies description and gives us a glimpse of what God is really like. I remember praying with a friend and being so aware of the glory of God that we both lost track of time. For days afterwards the

experience of 'real worship' lingered with me and enriched my life.

This is true worship! It happens when we recognize
who God is, and join the great company of heaven before the throne of God, declaring:

'Amen! Praise, glory, wisdom, thanksgiving, honour,
power, and might belong to our God for ever and ever!
Amen!' (Rev 7:12).

WORKSHOP SESSION TWO

Starter

Think praise

Form into groups of three. Each group is given a 'pretty
picture' from a magazine or calendar. Each picture
should depict some scene from nature: e.g. snow on
trees, waterfall, sunset, surf on beach.

Each group must discuss its picture and write a couple
of phrases of praise arising from the discussion. After a
few moments, the picture is passed on to another group,
and a new picture received.

The process is repeated four or five times. After about
ten minutes, the groups have to 'weld' their phrases together into a contemporary psalm which could be used in
worship.

Describe beautiful scenes you have known during your
life. Have you ever stopped at a wonderful scene or view
and praised God for what you saw?

Activity

Move in praise

In groups of three, construct a simple sequence of movements which depict one aspect of praise. Each group could be given a different word to work on: e.g. Awe, Wonder, Adoration, Love, Joy, 'Glory', or Worship.

Discuss your 'aspect of praise' and what you think it means. Share any times when you have experienced this kind of praise in worship.

Share with the other groups the different kinds of movement you have put together. The leader should then try to put together all of the contributions into one short piece of movement by the whole group.

A piece of music which is suitable for praise and worship should be played as the complete group moves together to glorify God. This activity will only work if the whole group is determined to experience together 'movement in praise'.

People who are blind, handicapped or immobile should be encouraged to participate in this. Some of the loveliest demonstrations of worship in our movement groups have come from Christians who are wheelchair-bound!

Question raiser

If you were faced with a congregation that 'didn't know how to praise', what would you do? In groups of three structure a programme of activities in your church for use before worship and during worship that you think might help.

Share your lists together.

Discuss together if any of these ideas would be helpful within your own church.

Discussion questions

1. 'I will praise thee with my whole heart' (Ps 138: 1av). Is it important to arrive at church early? What do we do if circumstances prevent us from arriving early?
2. Is kneeling important in worship? What kind of attitude does kneeling reveal?
3. Would you find it difficult to 'rage and act foolishly' in worship? Does this style of worship only appeal to some people? What are its dangers?
4. How would you rate the singing in your church? Is it really *zamar* praise?
   If not, what can be done?
5. How can we prepare ourselves for worship, so that we come full of expectation that we will 'glimpse God's glory'?

Closing prayers

Share together the 'movement' worked on earlier in the session. This time, the movement is an act of worship and not a demonstration. Each person in the group should try to put all his or her feelings into the movement so that it is a genuine expression of praise.

Gather in a circle, and hear the contemporary 'psalms' which were written by the group earlier in the session. After they have been read, pause in silence and look at the pictures on the floor in the centre of the circle.

Close by singing a simple song with *zamar* praise!

3

Where Two or Three Are Gathered

The Temple of Israel

I stood with my face almost touching the Western Wall (known to some as the Wailing Wall) in Jerusalem. It was the sabbath before Passover, and hundreds of Jews were praying there. Groups of men gathered at tables around open scrolls. Others bowed repeatedly toward the wall as they prayed or chanted. The noise of devotion filled the air. It was a very moving experience.

We were all standing and facing what was once the wall of the Temple. It is the spot where Jews from all over the world gather to remember the Holy Place, and to pray for the day when it will be theirs again.

As I closed my eyes and listened, I imagined myself in the Temple courts of Jesus' time. It would have been very similar, with the hum of worship all around. My studies about the Temple leapt to life.

I imagined the Outer Court, with its ornate colonnaded porches. This was the place where Gentiles were allowed to gather and where the money-changers and salespeople set up shop. I thought of the *Soreg*, the balustrade which separated this Court from the 'Inner Temple'. Gentiles like me were forbidden to cross the area on the penalty of death.

Beyond was the Inner Temple wall—built like a fortress with tall towers, gates, and a rampart. At the centre was the Beautiful Gate where Peter and John healed the lame beggar. This gate led into the Women's Court, with its beautiful galleries and porticoes, and its store-houses for wood and oil.

Beyond was the Gate of Nicanor leading into the Innermost Court. Only Jewish men were allowed to walk up the fifteen curved steps where the Levites used to sing, and go through Nicanor's Gate into the Court of the Israelites. Beyond this lay the Court for the Priests; and rising beyond it was the Holy of Holies.

The Holy of Holies was beautifully decorated with reddish marble columns. It was ornately gilded and crowned with ornaments. The walls were made of pure white marble. The historian Josephus described it as 'a snowy mountain glittering in the sun'. This square building represented the very heart of Jewish devotion and worship. It housed the Ark of the Covenant, and could only be entered by the High Priest one day each year.

As I opened my eyes and looked at the Western Wall it seemed to epitomize the Temple. A series of walls! Walls to keep out Gentiles, walls to keep out women, walls to keep out men, walls to keep out priests; a God behind walls, and hidden behind the great curtain of the Holy of Holies. The words of Hebrews came alive in a new way: 'We have then, my brothers, complete freedom to go into the Most Holy Place by means of the death of Jesus. He opened for us a new way, a living way, through the curtain—that is, through his own body'

(Heb 10:19–21).

Through his sacrificial death on the cross, Jesus opened the way for us to approach the Father. For the Christian worshipper there are no walls, no barriers and no balustrades. He has given us access! 'It was about twelve o'clock when the sun stopped shining and darkness covered the whole country until three o'clock; and the curtain hanging in the Temple was torn in two' (Lk 23:44). The walls are down, the door is open, the curtain is torn in two—the way is clear! No wonder Paul wanted the Ephesians to enter the joy of this experience! 'It is through Christ that all of us, Jews and Gentiles, are able to come in the one Spirit into the presence of the Father' (Eph 2:18; cf. 2:13–18).

Yet for many of us the 'walls of partition' have not been broken down. When we come to worship we remain in the Outer Courtyard of the Gentiles—out amid the noise of the money-changers and the salespeople and the clatter of comings and goings.

We have not realized that the gates are open, that the way is clear for us to walk through all the outer courtyards and into the Holy of Holies, into the very presence of the Most High God.

I see the 'people of the Outer Courtyard' in almost every congregation I visit. Their faces often betray their thoughts. Some people frankly admit that even here, in worship, God is far away.

I see people like the young man who times each service. He glances at his watch and assesses how much of the service is past and how much is yet to come. And woe to the preacher who lets the service run over the hour! Or like the church steward who confessed that his mind was always preoccupied with 'organization'. He counted the congregation, noted who was missing—and tried to remember who to give messages to at the end of the service.

A housewife admitted that her mind drifts towards the kitchen. Sunday lunch is an important event in her house, and she often wonders if she's set the cooker right. An accountant told me that he often added, subtracted and multiplied the hymn numbers in his head as the service progressed. His mind frequently reeled under complex mathematical puzzles that he set himself during the service.

The boy, eyeing up the girl in the youth group; the lay preacher, weighing up the vicar's theology; the organist, flicking through her hymnbook; the old man in the corner, sleeping peacefully. These are the people of the Outer Courtyard, those for whom the walls of partition still remain intact. God is far away, locked safely in the Holy of Holies, and truly inaccessible.

And I know that I am guilty, too. One Sunday, after a particularly stressful morning with the children, we slid into the pew with just a minute to spare.

I'd been making the toast, telling the children to get ready, trying to straighten up the house, and listen to the radio. I was wound up, fed up and het up before the service began.

The church was full. The hymns were joyful. The prayers were deep. The message was powerful. Yet I remained unmoved. I left the pew as empty as when I'd entered it. I'd been in church but I hadn't been at worship. I had lingered at the Outer Court. I hadn't entered the Holy Place.

The truth of the matter is that I often find it easier to worship when I'm leading a service than when I'm in the congregation. The reason is simple. When I am preaching at a service I usually spend at least an hour preparing myself beforehand. I check the hymns, look over the readings, meditate on the prayers and study the word.

By the time I get to church I'm ready for worship. From the first hymn I'm prepared to meet the living God.

But when I'm not preaching I tend to expect the minister to 'stir me'. I hope that the hymns will 'lift me'. I rely on the people in the fellowship to 'warm me'. I want the worship to 'bless me'.

Multiply this effect on the worship by ten if there are ten 'dead' worshippers present, twenty if there are twenty, or a hundred if there are a hundred, and the effect is startling! Leading worship in these circumstances can only be compared to dragging a heavy cart up a hill.

When people point at a church and say 'The worship there is dead', they imply that the fault lies with the minister—who's 'not lively enough'. Or they blame the music director who's 'behind the times'. Or they criticize the liturgy—which 'isn't contemporary'. But the truth of the matter is that dead worship is usually produced by dead congregations. No matter what is done to 'liven things up' it won't have the slightest effect until individual members of the congregation come to worship with a new attitude. They need to get serious about praising God!

The new Temple

Many Christians seem to treat the local church a bit like a Temple! They go to the Holy Place to sing their hymns, say their prayers and read God's word.

But that isn't New Testament thinking. Paul made it clear to the people in Corinth that the new Temple isn't a building—it's within the hearts, minds and souls of every believer. He wrote: 'Don't you know that your body is the temple of the Holy Spirit, who lives in you and was given to you by God? You do not belong to yourselves but to God; he bought you for a price. So use your bodies for God's glory' (1 Cor 6:19–20).

Here is the key to 'live' worship! It is when each believer gathered in church has ensured that the worship within his or her own being is really alive! When each worshipper is 'alive', corporate worship can't fail to live! Our worship depends on our relationship with the Lord Jesus Christ. If this is wrong, it's little wonder that our worship is dead! We need to ensure that our lives are under his lordship.

I have sometimes found myself counselling church members who have never received Christ into their lives as Lord and Saviour. No wonder they've found worship a bore! One night a man in his early seventies who had attended church throughout his life confessed his need to know Jesus. 'Am I too old?' he asked. I assured him that he wasn't! We can never fully participate in worship if Christ isn't at the centre of who we are. If we haven't trusted him to forgive us our sins and to cleanse us from our past, we can't possibly enter into the wonder of his presence.

Jesus promised 'I will be with you always, to the end of the age' (Mt 28:20). He is with us at home, at work and in all our journeying. We should spend time with him each day in prayer, building on the relationship we share. Jesus Christ should be someone who we count as our closest friend. He walks with us through all our joys and sorrows. He guides us, challenges us and strengthens us. When we enter the doors of our local church we are taking our living Saviour in with us! He is our priest and intercessor, and we are going to share our living relationship with the rest of the fellowship. The writer to the Hebrews reminds us of the right attitude!

So then, let us rid ourselves of everything that gets in the way, and of the sin which holds on to us so tightly, and let us run with determination the race that lies before us. Let us keep our eyes fixed on Jesus, on whom our faith depends from beginning to end (Heb 12:1–2).

When a congregation gathers to meet the living Jesus Christ, worship really does come alive! We can struggle with 'livening up worship', we can set up national commissions and local consultations to our heart's content. But the greatest priority is to develop congregations with a deeper spiritual life to share with one another.

When groups of spiritually alive believers gather together, the promise of Jesus is fulfilled. For he said; 'Where two or three come together in my name, I am there with them' (Mt 18:20). This is the true dynamic of live worship! Where Christians who have shared with him personally through the previous week gather for worship—*he is there*! The format of the worship is of secondary importance. No wonder St Paul wrote:

> 'You are . . . God's building. Using the gift that God gave me, I did the work of an expert builder and laid the foundation, and another man is building on it. But each man must be careful how he builds. For God has already placed Jesus Christ as the one and only foundation, and no other foundation can be laid' (1 Cor 3:10–11).

We haven't come together to 'sing some hymns'—but to sing praise to Jesus. We've not gathered to 'say some prayers'—but to talk to the living Christ. We've not gone to church to 'hear a sermon'—but to listen to Christ's word to us!

Even a handful of people worshipping with this attitude can really affect a huge congregation. I can see it in the eyes! Where there are sparkling, joyous eyes eager for teaching—I sense the presence of Christ. I can see it in the fellowship. Where people greet each other with a genuine warmth and love—I sense the presence of Christ.

The first priority in renewing worship is to look at the spiritual life of the individual members. By breaking down a congregation into groups of three or four and asking them to meet regularly to pray for each other's spiritual life, much will be achieved. As they pray for each other, they should ask for the renewing power of the Holy Spirit to sweep away the cobwebs and bring in a new spirit of praise.

Many Christians have gone to church faithfully for many years, but cannot recall a time when the presence of Christ was apparent in worship. This is tragic, for we should meet him every Sunday. Many of us are genuinely surprised when the sense of his presence in worship overwhelms us!

One godly minister whom I greatly respect recently told me of a special experience in worship some years ago. Half-way through his sermon he became aware of the presence of Christ in the church. He was deeply moved, and found it hard to concentrate on the rest of the service. After the service, he quietly made his way home. The sense of Christ's presence lingered with him for some days. People from the congregation telephoned to say that they had also met Christ in a special way.

This shouldn't be a once-in-a-lifetime experience. It should be the norm of Christian worship. Paul wrote, 'For we fix our attention, not on things that are seen, but on things that are unseen. What can be seen lasts only for a time, but what cannot be seen lasts for ever' (2 Cor 4:18).

The new priesthood

Even in the most 'low-church' congregations it is

possible to find a great reliance on 'experts' in worship. Worship, it is accepted, is the domain of those who have been to Bible College, the ordained, or the specially trained. They know how to do it properly. So when you invite someone in the congregation to give a reading or lead in prayer, they say 'I'm not good enough.'

Peter believed in the priesthood of all believers. He wrote:

> Come as living stones, and let yourselves be used in building the spiritual temple, where you will serve as holy priests to offer spiritual and acceptable sacrifices to God through Jesus Christ (1 Pet 2:5).

Although preachers and ministers have specific roles in the life of the church we are all supposed to fulfil a priestly role. We come with the authority to approach the Holy Place and to offer worship acceptable to the Lord. Instead of relying on others to fulfil a priestly role in leading us to God, we should be exercising that role ourselves! If we are not offering worship we are neglecting our function in the life of the church.

We can be the priests of the 'new Temple' by participating in worship in several ways. When I was on holiday in Holland I wanted to take my family to worship. We came across a group of Dutch Christians singing and praising God in the open air. We got into conversation with them, and they invited us to visit their church in Utrecht. We phoned to tell them we were on our way and they arranged for someone to meet us from the motorway and to lead us to the church. They arranged for our children to be taken into Sunday school—with their own interpreter! Older Christians sat beside us and translated the worship.

Everything seemed against us; a strange culture, a foreign language, and a two hour service. Yet the sense of living faith within that congregation is still with me. The people worshipped with such a depth of commitment and involvement that even if I hadn't understood a word—I would have been richly blessed.

This is the mystery of *faith*. I'm not sure how to describe it—except to say that when people come to church with a faith that overflows, it enriches worship. I believe there would be a new atmosphere in many church services if every participant asked God to give them a faith to bless and encourage everyone present. As we sing and pray and listen, we should be exercising a ministry of faith toward everyone else.

I also believe that every member of the new priesthood should offer a sacrifice of *praise*! We should come to offer praise to God irrespective of what anyone else is doing. Praise demands effort and energy. It is something springing from our innermost being. This 'sacrifice of praise' should not be hindered by our personal circumstances, swings of mood or spiritual highs or lows. It is something we give to the Lord.

As I looked down from the platform at a large convention meeting I saw a man in a wheelchair. He was grossly deformed with stumps for legs and badly twisted arms. He lay sprawled in the chair, his head lying on a pillow. As the worship continued I looked into his face. It looked like that of an angel. His beaming smile and sparkling eyes blessed me as he sang with all his heart. No matter what his personal circumstances, he had come as one of the 'new priesthood' to worship the Lord. His praise touched my heart and deeply challenged me.

I believe that the new priesthood should also offer a ministry of *prayer*. Not just when the preacher is leading in prayer, but throughout the service! I am so grateful that God has given me a team of Christians to travel on mission with me. Sometimes I have been ministering in hard situations—but have been very aware of the prayer support of my team. They are constantly in prayer, even when they are singing hymns or hearing the word. It makes a tremendous difference to worship to have people who are anointing it with the oil of intercession.

I feel sure that if congregations exercised their priestly responsibility of prayer, many services would really take off in a new way! It's not just the responsibility of the preacher to 'lead in prayer': We should all have a ministry of prayer in every service we attend.

And I believe that the new priesthood should demonstrate a ministry of *encouragement*. I find that I preach far more effectively if there are nods of approval, eyes that are alive with interest and voices that sometimes whisper 'Amen' or 'Hallelujah'. My leading of worship is impaired by stony stares, sour faces, and murmurs of disapproval. These things quench the Spirit and bring a mood of despair across the congregation. I believe that a handful of sour-faced worshippers can kill the praise of the liveliest congregations.

A worshipper who is critical, bored or inattentive is hardly exercising a priestly ministry. Such wrongful attitudes are sinful and destructive and lead to some churches being considered 'dead'.

The new priesthood must also exercise a ministry of *fellowship*. Where would Saul of Tarsus have been without the loving witness of Ananias who explained the gospel to him and baptized him? And how would he have gone on with the Lord without the encouragement of Barnabas, who brought him into the fellowship?

Fellowship is a spiritual ministry and is not to be confused with the efficient distribution of hymnbooks. Sometimes I have entered churches and been formally 'welcomed' by four different people and wanted to run a mile! This isn't fellowship. Fellowship comes naturally from the heart and spirit. It's not something we do once a month 'on the rota.' Nor is it a 'duty' we somehow get landed with. Fellowship is part of the priestly ministry of Christians toward each other and especially toward strangers.

If more people went to church to exercise a ministry of fellowship instead of 'waiting to be welcomed' things would be very different. As we give our love and friendship to those we meet at worship, we will be drawn closer together.

It irritates me when I look down from the pulpit and see that here and there throughout the congregation are people without hymnbooks. No one next to them, in front of them or behind them has noticed the fact! No one seems to care.

As we pray for those around us in worship and genuinely care for each other we will be exercising a ministry of fellowship. We are all members of the new priesthood and should be involved in making worship *live*—not only for ourselves, but for those around us.

It is easier to concentrate on the external formalities of worship. It is more personal and more painful to look at what goes on in our own hearts and minds. We should approach worship with a hunger and an expectancy that grows with the years. We should yearn to see him in all his resurrection glory, as John did on the Isle of Patmos:

> He held seven stars in his right hand, and a sharp two-edged sword came out of his mouth. His face was as bright as the midday sun. When I saw him, I fell down at his feet like a dead man. He placed his right hand on me and said, 'Don't be afraid! I am the first and the last. I am the *living one*.' (Rev 1:16–18).

It's time we came out of the Outer Courtyard and entered the Holy Place. It is time for worship to be our opportunity to meet the living God.

WORKSHOP SESSION THREE

Starter

The appointment

In groups of three work out a short mime to depict three people who are waiting for an appointment. All three are in a waiting room about to go in to the appointment.

Each group must role-play a different kind of appointment, and the others must guess who they are going in to see (e.g. a police interrogator, a dentist, a job interview).

Discuss: What kind of attitudes do people have when they have an appointment to go in to worship the living God? Are some of these attitudes wrong? What should our attitudes be?

Activity

The following objects are each placed before the group for about one minute. The group is asked to meditate on the person of Jesus Christ—using the object as the starting point for their thinking. The theme of this exercise is the verse: 'For we fix our attention, not on things that are seen, but on things that are unseen. What can be seen lasts only for a time, but what cannot be seen lasts for ever' (2 Cor 4:18).

1. A lighted candle—(Jesus is the light of the world).
2. A branch or leaf—(Jesus is the true vine).
3. A crust of bread—(Jesus is the bread of life).

Discuss: How can we take control of our thoughts and stop them from wandering during worship? How can we focus on 'things unseen' rather than seen? What practical advice and experience has each member of the group to share?

Question raiser

In groups of three, draw a series of four squares within each other. Mark the innermost square 'Holy of Holies'.

What kind of walls are there between each of us and the 'Holy Place'? Some of these walls may be self-erected barriers, others may be erected by the structure of the services. As a group, label the 'walls' with different reasons why worship is sometimes difficult.

Share our 'walls' together as a whole group. Discuss together ways in which they can be demolished!

Closing prayers

Read together Psalm 139:1–12. Imagine that you have come to worship without any sense of the presence of God. Which of the phrases in this psalm would you meditate on if the cause was:

1. Depression.
2. Failure.
3. Loneliness.
4. Doubt.

Using the ideas expressed in your discussion and the phrases selected from the psalm, share in open prayer together. Recognize before God that he is with us—even when we don't know it!

4
Breaking Bread

My wife and I and our two young children dived into the back pew during the first hymn. We were on holiday in Wales and had found difficulty in locating an English-speaking church. The elderly priest gave us an unwelcoming stare, and the dozen or so worshippers turned round to look at us as they sang. No one smiled at us, or helped us find which page to turn to. From the very beginning I felt decidedly uncomfortable! There were no other children present and I didn't feel that our family was particularly welcome.

I have nothing against the 1662 Prayer Book service, but the way it was read that morning spoilt its beauty and poetry. The priest droned on in a tired monotone. No one seemed involved. Gradually our children stopped wriggling. My wife and I made a space between us on the pew and they stretched out and went to sleep. Even I had to fight to keep awake, and I wondered when the service would ever end.

I recognize that worship relies on the participation of

worshippers, but I found it impossible to worship that morning. The liturgy was an intrusion into worship. The stale atmosphere and boring presentation alienated me from the Lord.

Afterwards one of the elderly ladies in the congregation complimented us on our 'well-behaved children'. I found it hard to keep a straight face. Most children are 'well behaved' when they're fast asleep!

I have also known charismatic worship intrude on my approach to God. Sometimes an insensitive use of the gifts of the Holy Spirit has made me ask, 'Is this honouring the Lord?'

I was leading the sacrament of Holy Communion at a huge charismatic gathering numbering several thousand people. There were no books, Bibles or printed service papers to hand. I had to 'busk' the Lord's Supper as best I could. As the service continued, I realized that there were too few servers to feed the congregation with bread and wine. We had to recruit people as the service continued and direct them from the platform!

The ensuing moments were a kind of slow-motion nightmare. As I tried to put together a spontaneous liturgy I also plotted how to direct the servers around the hall. During the distribution of the elements I felt like a car park attendant—waving people with bread and wine this way and that. By the end of the worship I was a nervous wreck. I felt I'd cheated the congregation. There had been a lack of dignity, a lack of order, and a lack of depth in the liturgy. We hadn't treated the sacrament with the reverence it deserved. The chaos hadn't honoured the Lord.

Liturgy is important. It isn't good enough to make up the service as we go along. The celebration of the Lord's Supper deserves thought and preparation.

I look back on these two bad experiences as 'markers'

for my own approach to leading the Communion Service. I am aware that if I use a set liturgy without imagination or life, it's like stale bread. But equally, if a celebration has no shape or order, it's like cheap wine with no body. People need freedom to worship in spirit; they need order to worship in truth.

Right from the earliest days of church history this kind of 'mix' has been apparent. In AD 150, Justin Martyr wrote:

> At the end of the prayers, we greet one another with a kiss. Then the president of the brethren is brought bread and a cup of wine mixed with water; and he takes them, and offers up praise and glory to the Father of the universe, through the name of the Son and of the Holy Ghost, and gives thanks at considerable length for our being counted worthy to receive these things at his hands. When he has concluded the prayers and thanksgivings, all the people present express their joyful assent by saying 'Amen'. Then those whom we call deacons give to each of those present the bread and wine mixed with water over which the thanksgiving was pronounced, and carry away a portion to those who are absent' (*Apologia I*).

The Eucharist is not something we can 'play about with' at will. It is part of the rich tradition which has been passed down to us from Jesus Christ, and we must treat it with care.

When I was in theological college one 'angry young man' led us in a Eucharist using squash and biscuits. The whole thing seemed too trendy and gimmicky to be taken seriously. The tutor next to me muttered loudly 'Oh what fun . . . it's like the teddy bears' picnic!' We dishonour God if we make the Eucharist approachable but lose its meaning.

Rediscovering Passover

I believe that the Last Supper occurred on Passover night, and that much of the significance of Christ's words can only be understood in that context. In order to understand the rich meaning of Christ's words at the Last Supper, we need to rediscover Passover. As we recognize the undertones which flowed beneath the Passover celebration, we can appreciate the full force of what Jesus was doing.

The Passover meal was a celebration of the miraculous way in which Israel was set free from slavery in Egypt. God instructed the people to eat the Passover meal on that historic night when they were saved from plague. The following morning they began their pilgrimage through the Red Sea and on through the wilderness to the Promised Land.

As Jesus and his disciples gathered in the Upper Room their minds would have been full of past Passover celebrations. They would have been aware of its significance to them as part of the people of Israel under the guiding hand of God. Under the Roman domination of their day the Passover would have taken on even more significance.

One Passover night in Israel, I went to a Passover meal where a Jewish expert described what would have happened during the Last Supper. First Jesus would have taken the 'Cup of Kiddush' and prayed over it. This was a symbolic act at the start of the celebration. As the cup was passed from disciple to disciple, it would have reminded them that this was no ordinary meal. It was something set apart and made holy by the will of almighty God.

Jesus would then have washed his hands three times in the prescribed way as a sign that he was to preside over the Passover feast. Then he would have taken a piece of hyssop (parsley) and dipped it into a bowl of salt water, while the others did the same. This would have been a poignant moment, for it symbolized the hyssop that was dipped in blood and used to paint the doorposts, that night of Passover long before. The bowl of salt water would have reminded them of the tears of the years of slavery in Egypt, and the salt waters of the Red Sea. Only hours later Jesus was offered a sponge stuck on the end of a hyssop branch when he hung on the Cross. Hyssop signified deliverance.

Jesus would have broken the first loaf and blessed it. Only a little of this loaf would have been eaten. It was a stinging reminder that the slaves in Egypt never had a whole loaf, only stale crusts. As he broke the bread Jesus would have said: 'This is the bread of affliction which our forefathers ate in the land of Egypt. Whoever is hungry let him come and eat. Whoever is in need let him come and keep the Passover with us.' They are great words of invitation, which are echoed in the words of the Eucharist today.

As was the custom, the youngest person at the table would have asked Jesus to explain the Passover. Jesus then probably recited the history of God's dealings with Israel and the story of their deliverance from Egypt. The disciples would have sung the great psalms of deliverance (Psalm 113 and 114), and the 'Cup of Haggadah' (of 'explaining') would have been passed around. Next, probably, everyone washed their hands, Jesus said grace, and the meal could begin.

Small pieces of unleavened bread would have been passed among the disciples. This was an important reminder that the people of Israel had been told to prepare for the journey by packing unleavened dough in baking pans.

The disciples would have placed bitter herbs between pieces of unleavened bread and dipped it into the sauce. This was called a 'sop', and the bitter tasting flavour reminded them of the anguish and suffering which the people of Israel endured while they were making bricks from straw for their Egyptian masters.

The disciples then probably ate the Passover lamb. It symbolized the spilling of blood that was necessary so that the doorposts could be daubed, and reminded them of the way that the people of Israel were delivered.

After the lamb was eaten, Jesus would have passed round the remainder of the unleavened bread and declared, 'Take and eat—this is my body.' Then he would have said the prayer of thanksgiving which looked with anticipation to the coming Messiah. Jesus probably chose this moment as the time for instituting the 'memorial feast'; 'This is my body, broken for you.' Jesus then passed the cup of thanksgiving to the disciples and invested this simple act with new meaning as he declared: 'Drink it, all of you—this is my blood, which seals God's covenant.'

This covenant went back to the dawn of Jewish history. God appeared to Abraham, to Isaac and then to Jacob and declared that their people would become a mighty nation and would possess the land of Canaan. He also appeared to Moses with the same promise just before the first Passover.

During this celebration of the Old Covenant, Jesus announced the New Covenant! He declared that his blood represented the sealing of a new covenant for the 'new Israel'—the church. Hebrews summed it up:

> Christ is the one who arranges a new covenant, so that those who have been called by God may receive the eternal blessings that God has promised. This can be done because there has been a death which sets people free from the

wrongs they did whilst the first covenant was in force (Heb 9:15).

After singing a hymn the Passover ended, and Jesus led his disciples to the Mount of Olives and on into Gethsemane. Soon he was dragged toward Calvary, where the New Covenant was sealed for ever.

The meal of the kingdom

The Passover meal was a meal of the kingdom. It was the last meal the people of Israel celebrated under slavery in Egypt. They were not to celebrate Passover again until the long years of pilgrimage were over and they had reached the Promised Land. It was a meal that became the focus of hope as they marched through the wilderness to the Promised Land.

The Eucharist is a meal of the new kingdom. As we read the familiar words of Jesus, 'I tell you, I will never again drink this wine until the day I drink the new wine with you in my Father's Kingdom' (Mt 26:29), we are making the Eucharist the focus of our hope, and we look forward to the time when we will share the great banquet of praise with him in his new kingdom.

At the Lord's table we may be a people of different ethnic backgrounds, ages, socio-economic groups, and educational backgrounds. But at this table we are one people, one community, one kingdom—and we are all awaiting one coming king.

As I move along the line of worshippers with hands outstretched to receive the bread I am often moved. As I place the bread into hand after hand I look at the different outstretched hands. Black hands and white hands; some wrinkled with age, others young and smooth. Hands gnarled by work. Hands twisted by arthritis. Hands open to receive. This is the kingdom community, and there are no divisions here!

The Bread of Life

The Passover meal used unleavened bread. It was a reminder that at the first Passover, everyone had their baking pans full of unleavened dough ready for the journey ahead. They would need to travel many days on the sustenance of this unleavened bread. As Jesus took the unleavened bread and shared it among them their minds must have flashed back to when he said:

> What Moses gave you was not the bread from heaven; it is my Father who gives you the real bread from heaven. For the bread that God gives is he who comes down from heaven and gives life to the world . . . I am the bread of life . . . he who comes to me will never be hungry (Jn 6:32–33, 35).

As we take the bread in our hands we know we've come to feed on the Bread of Life. As it becomes part of us, we are absorbing his life into our own. As we draw physical strength from bread we draw spiritual strength from Jesus—The Bread of Life.

As the people of Israel left the first Passover meal they marched out into the wilderness in the strength of their unleavened bread. As we rise from the Lord's Table, we know that his strength will be sufficient for us in whatever wilderness we may be called to travel.

In a little chapel on a large London council estate, we celebrated the Eucharist on the first Sunday evening of the month. There were only a handful of worshippers and most of them were handicapped and elderly. The church steward used to put out a row of chairs by the communion rail so that they could sit while they received the elements.

There was nothing very contemporary about our simple celebration together. We used the Prayer Book service, but gave space for open prayer. Sometimes I was so aware of the Lord's presence with us that I forgot what to do next! The liturgy had carried us to the throne of God.

As the communicants moved slowly back to the centre of the church, I could sense that something had changed. They still hobbled, most of them bowed down by age. They were still returning to times of hardship and difficulty back home. They still faced the prospect of lonely days 'shut in' from the world. Yet, mysteriously, Christ had been made known to them afresh in the breaking of bread. And in the sure knowledge of the truth, they would have strength for whatever lay ahead.

The blood of Christ

The Feast of Passover demanded a sacrifice. The young lambs were killed—and they had to be without spot or blemish. Their blood was used to daub the lintels and doorposts as a sign that these households were to be saved. The Passover lambs were to be eaten as the main course of the meal, and not a scrap was to be kept.

Paul wrote: 'For our Passover Festival is ready, now that Christ, our Passover lamb, has been sacrificed' (1 Cor 5:7). The Eucharist is a living symbol of Christ's sacrifice for us. Paul made it clear that whenever the Eucharist is celebrated, we must remember Christ's redeeming death.

I don't pretend to comprehend the complex theological arguments concerning the Eucharist. What I do know is that whenever I drink the wine I picture the cross and remember Christ's death on Calvary for me. I know again that I can never work my way to heaven. My salvation rests on One who died so that I could be forgiven.

> When Christ went through the tent and entered once and for all into the Most Holy Place, he did not take the blood of goats and bulls to offer as a sacrifice; rather, he took his own blood and obtained eternal salvation for us (Hebrews 9:12).

The Eucharist is a wonderful reminder to all of us that Jesus gave his life blood for our salvation. As the cup is lifted high and passed among the people, we should ask ourselves:

> And can it be that I should gain
> An interest in the Saviour's blood?
> Died he for me, who caused his pain?
> For me, who him to death pursued?
> Amazing love! How can it be
> That thou, my God shouldst die for me?

WORKSHOP SESSION FOUR

Starter

Packing your bags

The group is asked to pretend that after the meeting they are going on a long journey together—never to return! Each person must come to the group with a suitcase containing three precious possessions. Open your suitcases and share your possessions together.

Each person must explain why they chose these three things.

Talk about how the people of Israel must have felt on Passover night, just before they left Egypt to start the pilgrimage toward the Promised Land. Do you ever feel as though you're on a pilgrimage?

Activity

The storyteller

One of the highlights of Passover celebration was the storytelling. The youngest person in the group asked the leader why they were celebrating the Passover, and the leader told the story of God's dealings with Israel.

Divide into groups of four. Imagine that a young person has asked you to explain the Eucharist. The group must tell the story of how the Last Supper came about. The group may choose any of these methods of recounting the story:

1. Drama.
2. Interview of 'eyewitnesses'.
3. Poetry.
4. A news bulletin.
5. Simple storytelling—each person in the group sharing a different segment.

Gather back together and hear the 'story' from the different groups.

Question raiser

In the third century AD Hippolytus said that Holy Communion should be the first food of the day. For many centuries, Christians were expected to fast through the day until they received the bread and wine. This fast could only be dispensed with under very exceptional circumstances. It is only in this present century (notably after 1957), that the Roman Catholic church has relaxed its rules on this.

Do you think it would be a good thing to fast before communion?

Do we treat the sacrament too lightly today? If so, why?

In which ways should we prepare ourselves to take the Eucharist?

Discussion questions (To be discussed either as a whole group or in sub-groups)

Read together: 1 Corinthians 11:17–34.
Discuss this passage. Then answer the following questions:
1. 'I do not praise you, because your meetings for worship actually do more harm than good' (v.17). Is there any sense in which our celebration of the Lord's Supper could do harm? Give examples.
2. 'The Lord Jesus, on the night he was betrayed, took a piece of bread, gave thanks to God, broke it, and said, "This is my body, which is for you. Do this in memory of me"' (vv.23–24). How would you improve the liturgy of Eucharist to enhance its meaning?
3. 'In the same way, after the supper he took the cup and said, "This cup is God's new covenant, sealed with my blood. Whenever you drink it, do so in memory of me"' (v.25). Most celebrations of the Eucharist incorporate periods of silence for personal prayer and meditation. What should we think of in these spaces, and how can we best use these pools of silence? Share ideas together.
4. 'This means that every time you eat this bread and drink from this cup you proclaim the Lord's death until he comes' (v.26). The Eucharist should be a celebration of hope that one day we will share the heavenly banquet. How can we bring this message home to people?

Closing prayers

Celebrate a simple Eucharist together. If your church or denomination requires the vicar or elder to preside at the celebration please ensure that this is done.

Discuss with the leadership of your church a simple form of 'house communion' for those who will take part. Make sure that there are plenty of spaces in the celebration for personal prayer and meditation, so that the meaning of this session can be emphasized.

5

The Foolishness of Preaching

'It'll never work,' I said. 'The days when thousands of people will stand in the cold and listen to a preacher are long gone.' My rather sarcastic jibe went down like a lead balloon—particularly as it was my first appearance at the central concept committee of Mission England.

I was being honest. I wasn't convinced that thousands of people would fill football stadiums all over the country to hear an elderly American preacher called Billy Graham. The other members of the committee convinced me that it was worth a try, though I lived with a tinge of scepticism until the crusade began.

I've been eating my words ever since! Mission England proved without doubt that the age of preaching is not dead. People flocked to the football grounds in their thousands, and for many of them it was the moment of decision to follow Christ.

As I sat on the stadium platform in Villa Park and looked around at that vast congregation all the months of committees in which I'd been involved suddenly seemed worthwhile.

As Cliff Barrows conducted the choir and congregation in his own inimitable style the telephone near the lectern began to ring. Cliff reached down and took the phone. 'It's Billy,' he whispered to us. 'He's stuck in a traffic jam miles away—I guess we'd better carry on singing!'

Eventually I heard the roar of police sirens and the evangelist arrived. Within minutes he was at the lectern preaching, and the huge congregation was hushed and silent as they hung on his every word. I sat and looked around the terraces of the stadium as the evangelist continued. There were no gimmicks or signs of emotionalism. Here was one man preaching the old gospel story, and people were spellbound by what they heard.

That afternoon, countless lives were changed as hundreds of people swarmed on to the pitch to give their hearts to Christ. A harvest was reaped. I realized afresh that the simple power of the preached word should never be underestimated. Over recent years it has been derided, mocked and even despised—yet it is still used by God in a mighty way.

As a Methodist I look back to the eighteenth-century revival with great affection. As it swept through the country there were many demonstrations of the power of preaching. Time and time again God used the simple power of the preacher to influence vast numbers of people. Open air preaching became necessary when George Whitefield was forbidden to preach in St Mary's Church in Islington. He decided to hold an open air meeting in a park called Moorfields. It was a rough place where crowds gathered each evening for bear-baiting, wrestling, cudgel playing and dog fights. The account of his first open air meeting on the site reads:

Public notice having been given . . . upon coming out of the coach he found an incredible number of people assembled. Many had told him that he should never come again out of that place alive. He went in, however, between two of his friends, who, by the pressure of the crowd were soon parted entirely from him and were obliged to leave him at the mercy of the rabble. But these, instead of hurting him, formed a lane for him and carried him along to the middle of the fields . . . from whence he preached without molestation to an exceedingly great multitude (*Gillies Journal*).

The meetings grew more and more popular, until tens of thousands of people were gathering night after night to hear the preaching of this twenty-four year old parson. Soon the meetings were held in Kennington to provide more space, and on Sunday, May 6th 1739 Whitefield's diary reads:

At six preached at Kennington. Such a sight I never saw before. I believe there were no less than fifty thousand people, and near four score coaches, besides great numbers of horses . . . God gave me great enlargement of heart. I continued my discourse for an hour and a half, and when I returned home, I was filled with such love, peace and joy that I cannot express it (*Whitefield's Journals*).

Occasional references from journals of the late 1730s give us an idea of what his sermons were like. One day, for instance, Whitefield preached to a vast crowd about a blind man with a dog walking on the brink of a precipice. Whitefield described this scene with such detail that the congregation sat with bated breath. Lord Chesterfield, who was in the congregation, stood up and shouted 'Good God! The man's gone!' 'No, my Lord,' answered Whitefield, 'he is not quite gone; let us hope that he may be saved.' He went on to describe the danger of trusting in our own blind direction instead of trusting in the love of Jesus Christ. This sense of urgency and passionate appeal was obviously a hallmark of Whitefield's preaching.

Soon John and Charles Wesley joined him in this exciting ministry. Charles Wesley found it spiritually and emotionally draining. In a letter to Whitefield he wrote, 'I am continually tempted to leave off preaching, and hide myself . . . Do not reckon upon me, brother, in the work God is doing, for I cannot expect He should long employ one who is ever longing and murmuring to be discharged.'

This fear and reticence was certainly not obvious to his congregations in the open air. Joseph Williams of Kidderminster wrote down his impressions of Charles Wesley preaching in the open air.

> I found him, standing on a table board in an erect posture, with his hands and eyes lifted up to heaven in prayer with uncommon fervency, fluency, and variety of proper expressions. He then preached about an hour in such a manner as I scarce ever heard any man preach. Though I have heard many a finer sermon, according to the common taste . . . I never heard any man discover such evident signs of a vehement desire, or labour so earnestly to convince his hearers that they were all by nature in a sinful, lost, undone state . . . He showed how great a change a faith in Christ would produce in the whole man.

Moving further back in history, it is important to notice how crucial the work of the preacher was in the life of the early church. The power and passion of Peter's preaching at Pentecost was dynamic. We read in Acts:

> Peter made his appeal to them and with many other words he urged them, saying, 'Save yourselves from the punishment coming on this wicked people!' Many of them believed his message and were baptized, and about three thousand people were added to the group that day (Acts 2:40–41).

As I sat on the hill overlooking Galilee where Jesus is

thought to have preached his Sermon on the Mount, I imagined what it must have been like. There in the open air without amplification he exclaimed . . . 'You are like salt for all mankind. But if salt loses its saltiness, there is no way to make it salty again' (Mt 5:13). It must have been a powerful message.

It is time for us to reassert the importance of the preached word. Too many preachers have replaced the ministry of proclamation with the delivery of short homilies. These sermons say little, disturb no one, and lack any real dynamic. People's lives are not challenged or changed, the Bible remains closed, and the power of God is not evident within them.

Many people have come to assume that preaching is second best, old fashioned, and irrelevant to contemporary society. We need to pray that there will be a new confidence in the preached word! Time and again through history, the Lord has used the force of a single human voice to turn the hearts of men and women back to him. We must not look down on the place of preaching in worship, for it is the part of the service in which we receive what God has for us. We listen for his word to us—and our prayer is—'Speak to me!' Paul reminded us:

> But how can they call to him for help if they had not believed? And how can they believe if they had not heard the message? And how can they hear if the message is not proclaimed? And how can the message be proclaimed if the messengers are not sent out? As the scripture says, 'How wonderful is the coming of messengers who bring good news!' (Rom 10:14–15).

Although much of my work in recent years has been connected with the renewal of worship, I have never downgraded preaching! It disturbs me when I hear of services where there is movement, music, drama and art—but no preaching! Although I am committed to the use of these forms in worship I don't see them as replacing the role of the preacher. Far from it, the preached word often clinches what God has been saying throughout the service. I want to see more preaching, not less!

The role of the congregation

One of my favourite comedy records is Alan Bennett's 'Beyond the Fringe' sketch called 'Take a Pew'. It is a send-up of all the bad habits which preachers seem to develop; the constant repetition of unimportant phrases, the parsonical voice, and the inept illustration. I have played this record to groups of preachers in different parts of the country. It's a hopeful sign, that some of them laughed! It was even more encouraging to hear many of them admit that they could hear themselves in the sketch—I only hope it made them think about their style.

It's easy for us to make fun of preachers. There have been occasions when I've struggled to keep a straight face! Yet we all have a responsibility towards those who preach the word and we have a duty to give them helpful encouragement. There is nothing more irritating than hearing people say 'Nice sermon, Minister' when you're pretty sure they didn't like it at all. I've been quite devastated by negative criticism about my preaching, but I've found constructive comments very helpful. Congregations deserve the preachers that they get. Unless they take positive steps to help their preachers improve, how can anything change?

When I was a student at Cliff College, we used to have a weekly meeting called 'The Sermon Clinic'. The victim would mount the pulpit steps in fear and trepidation to preach while the college community took copious notes.

Each student had a questionnaire to fill in, and after the sermon was over they gathered in groups to discuss it. I remember sitting before the college community to hear the 'report back' on my sermon. It was a frightening experience, and I felt a bit like a prisoner in court as the reports were read out. But it was all done with great care and sensitivity and I have found the comments very helpful since.

Many preachers would welcome constructive comeback from their preaching. They want to serve the Lord more effectively and would appreciate friendly advice in order to develop their ministry. Bear in mind however, that we preachers are sensitive animals and that some of us might give up if the criticism is too harsh!

Congregations also have a responsibility to pray for those who bring the word. In some Methodist Circuits which cover fifteen or twenty chapels, many people use the preaching plan as a prayer list. This is a real encouragement to the preachers who can be assured of prayer during their preparation as well as when they preach.

I've always been encouraged when groups of people have gathered before a service to pray for me. I have felt the difference it makes. When I'm in the vestry before a service, it's so good to have godly folk to pray for me and to support me spiritually. When I am on mission I thank God for my team who assure me that they are praying for me as I preach. Preaching is sometimes like spiritual warfare—and prayer support is a very great encouragement.

We can also influence a preacher by the manner in which we listen. I have preached in some churches and sensed a real barrier to communication. The folk in the pew seem determined to reject what I have brought for them. I can read it in their posture, their eyes, and their restlessness. I can take the same sermon to another church and find that the hushed concentration liberates me, and the eagerness on people's faces draws the word out of me!

Jesus quoted from Isaiah when he was teaching his disciples about preaching. He said:

> This people will listen and listen, but not understand; they will look and look, but not see, because their minds are dull, and they have stopped up their ears and have closed their eyes. Otherwise, their eyes would see, their ears would hear, their minds would understand, and they would turn to me, says God, and I would heal them. (Mt 13:14–15).

As we sit in the pew we have a responsibility to prepare ourselves to hear the word that is brought to us. This demands a commitment to listen, an effort of concentration, and a hunger to receive from the word of God. We should look to the pulpit with eager anticipation asking, 'What does the Lord want to say to me today?'

By taking our Bibles and following the references given we can focus our attention, and by taking notepads and biros we can visibly demonstrate that we mean business with the word of God. I know what it means to me when I see a congregation with Bibles open and biros at the ready. Here is a people who are ready to receive!

We need to prepare our hearts and minds so that we can receive the word! It is of little use being good listeners if we're not prepared to put into practice what we've heard. We must listen and be willing to change.

James exhorted the church with these words: 'But whoever looks closely into the perfect law that sets people free, who keeps on paying attention to it and does not simply listen to it and then forget it—but *puts it into practice*—that person will be blessed by God in what he does' (Jas 1:25, my italics).

There's no doubt in my mind that congregations have

a responsibility towards preachers. For too long many have 'switched off' at sermon time and have missed hearing God's word for them. A good prayer before a sermon would be Frances Ridley Havergal's famous hymn:

> Master speak! Thy servant heareth,
> Waiting for thy gracious word,
> Longing for thy voice that cheereth;
> Master, let it now be heard.
> I am listening, Lord for thee;
> What hast thou to say to me?

The role of the preacher

I believe that the role of the preacher needs to be redefined. In many churches the one who preaches also conducts the worship. I feel that this may well be wrong. The ministry of preaching is one gift, the ministry of leading praise and worship is another.

The situation is made worse when a preacher comes from a different town to preach in our church. The visitor doesn't know where the congregation is at in its worship. A lively congregation is constantly moving and developing in its worship life, and a stranger can't possibly pitch the worship at the right level. The visitor can't know about the church's music ministry, or appreciate what gifts can be released locally for participation in worship. He can't understand the prayer needs of the local community. He comes in with some hymns he has chosen and expects to lead the local people 'from cold'.

Leadership of praise and worship is a separate gift—and we should recognize those within the local Christian community who have the calling to fulfil it. Preaching is something different and we should look for those who are called to it wherever they are needed.

The church needs to recognize that there is a diverse range of preaching gifts. Those who teach and expound the word of God are not necessarily suited to preaching for conversion. Those who can use visual aids effectively with small children are not always able to communicate to teenagers.

We expect preachers to speak to a multiplicity of congregations and to adapt their style accordingly—but I've despaired as I've watched a minister struggling to talk to young children when it was plainly not his gift; or when I've heard a wonderful Bible expositor speaking to elderly working class women way 'above their heads'; or when I've seen a dignified elderly cleric try to be 'with it' and alienate a teenage congregation! Preachers should learn to recognize where their preaching gift lies—and how to use it accordingly.

Preaching is a vital and important ministry and many churches have grown lazy in their administration of it. Not only have we forced preachers into situations which were clearly 'not for them', we have sometimes allowed them to 'preach themselves dry'.

I find nothing scriptural about making ministers preach twice on Sundays year in and year out. I've done it, and I know the great emotional and spiritual strain it can be. It's little wonder that many ministers 'lose the fire' in their preaching—they have written too many new sermons and preached to the same congregation too often. They've no more to give.

On the other hand, some ministers grow proud and become wary of letting others into their pulpits. They feel indispensable, and are tempted to think of other preachers as inferior. Congregations would do well to reassure their ministers that they don't have to preach so often to 'earn their crust'. They should be part of a preaching team bringing the word of God to the congregation when they have a fresh message from the Lord.

Sadly, sermon preparation has become a burden for many preachers. Preaching has become a duty. Sermons have been turned out on a production line. The ministry of preaching has become a habit—not a happening.

Moreover, the preaching gift is a gift from God and it is not given to everyone. Perhaps some preachers are not supposed to be preachers at all but have been pressed into the work for the wrong reasons. Unfortunately congregations are having to suffer the consequences.

Paul wrote:

> So the one who came down is the same one who went up, above and beyond the heavens, to fill the whole universe with his presence. It was he who 'gave gifts to mankind'; he appointed some to be apostles, others to be prophets, others to be evangelists, others to be pastors and teachers (Eph 4:10–11).

Is the preacher next Sunday appointed by God or by man? We must never forget that preaching is a gift of the Spirit, not something we can learn from a book!

The language barrier

Sometimes I've sat in church and been aware that people aren't listening to the sermon. Of course, there's no real way of knowing, but the distant eyes and stony faces are a fair indication that people aren't really 'with' the preacher.

I can't believe that the people looked like this when Jesus gave his Sermon on the Mount. I don't think that the crowd was daydreaming when Peter gave his famous Pentecost sermon, and I'm sure that Whitefield and the Wesleys managed to hold people's attention. Preachers are called by God, but they also need to put study and effort into improving their style.

Is it possible that we've lost the art of preaching, in many of our churches? Could it be that preaching as we know it is but a pale reflection of what our forefathers knew? Times have changed and the influence of television on communication skills has been dramatic. I'm afraid that in changing style to suit the modern age we've lost some important preaching techniques along the way. Is preaching a lost art?

Storytelling

One of the techniques that is useful to the preacher is the art of storytelling. The biography of the great Methodist preacher Dr Sangster describes his peculiar preaching style.

> He had a most unusual dramatic sense. It was not the polished skill of the actor, but a rarer gift—the vivid report, perfectly executed, of an eye-witness. It would not be true to say he was a consummate actor in the pulpit; rather was it that his imagination had dwelt so intensely on what he was saying that he lived it and reproduced it—not 'Elijah did it like this', but 'here is Elijah doing it.'[1]

In many of the sermons I have heard, the art of storytelling is dead. We are treated to a diatribe of opinions, hypotheses and dogma—but there are no stories! Two thousand years ago, Jesus understood that to capture and hold people's attention he needed to tell stories. But many of us have not learnt the lesson. Good stories can grip people's attention and communicate meaning far more powerfully than a series of abstract statements. I love to hear preachers telling stories and making them live.

---

[1]From Paul Sangster, *Dr Sangster* (Epworth Press) by permission.

Simplicity

Some of the sermons that I have heard are complex reasoned statements. There is often an introduction, three points, and a conclusion. This is the style taught in theological colleges and in authoritative text books—but I don't sense that it was the preaching style of Jesus!

He spoke straight from the heart. Simply. Directly. To the point. He didn't build a complex superstructure of argument. He said what was on his mind.

I'm quite sure that many people get lost because sermons are too complicated. Most congregations are only able to receive one point from a sermon. Jesus's style was uncluttered, pithy and straightforward. I only wish some contemporary preachers would follow his example. Here is an example of his preaching style:

> Aren't five sparrows sold for two pennies? Yet not one sparrow is forgotten by God. Even the hairs of your head have all been counted. So do not be afraid; you are worth much more than many sparrows! (Lk 12:6–7).

Now, what could be simpler than that?

Urgency

Jesus' ministry began in urgency. His opening message was 'Turn away from your sins, because the Kingdom of heaven is near!' (Mt 4:17). The time was near, the kingdom was at hand, the message was urgent!

Yet many modern messages lack any hint of urgency. The preacher's calling is summed up in Paul's words: 'So we preach Christ to everyone. With all possible wisdom we warn and teach them in order to bring each one into God's presence as a mature individual in union with Christ' (Col 1:28).

I remember a Catholic priest striding up the church

aisle and knocking on the pews as he shouted 'Jesus says "I stand at the door and knock."' This was preaching with urgency! I wish some of the laid-back Protestant preachers could have seen it!

Any preacher who has looked down to where some friend was sitting last week—but has now died—knows that the message is still as urgent as ever.

Authority

The hallmark of Christ's preaching was authority. We read in Matthew's gospel: 'When Jesus finished saying these things, the crowd was amazed at the way he taught. He wasn't like the teachers of the Law; instead, he taught with authority' (Mt 7:28–29). I find this ingredient lacking in many of the sermons I hear today. Some preachers seem determined to press upon us their doubts and uncertainties rather than that of which they're sure. Some excellent advice given to me as a teenage preacher was, 'Preach faith! They've doubts enough!'

Once D. L. Moody was preaching to a rowdy group of university students. They were laughing at him and ruining the service in whatever way they could. Finally, Moody could take no more. 'You jeered at the hymns,' he exclaimed, 'and I said nothing. You jeered at the prayers and I said nothing. But now you jeer at the word of God. I would as soon play with forked lightning!'

The source of our authority doesn't lie in our political opinions, our 'true life experiences' or in our prejudices. It lies deep within the word of God. Sermons which are not Bible-based are not really sermons at all.

Paul defended his own ministry in Thessalonica, when he wrote:

> Our appeal to you is not based on error or impure motives, nor do we try to trick anyone. Instead, we always speak as

God wants us to, because he has judged us worthy to be entrusted with the Good News. We do not try to please men, but to please God, who tests our motives. (1 Thess 2:3–4).

Visual

I'm sure that the use of visual aids is something that every preacher should master. Jesus pointed to everyday things like mustard seeds, fruit trees, mountains, and vines when he spoke. His sermons were packed with visual references. Pictorial images and visual aids are rarely used in sermons today. Yet ask any group of people about the sermons they remember, and they will probably recall those with a visual element.

There is an ancient proverb which should challenge every preacher: 'I hear, I forget; I see, I remember.'

Brevity

Some people can preach effectively for an hour, others can't. Brevity isn't a sin!

Response

I recently heard a fine sermon in a large London church. It was clearly delivered, well prepared and beautifully illustrated. At the end of the sermon I wanted to leap up and ask—'What do you want us to do about it, then?' For there was no application, no demand for response, and nothing in my heart had changed as a result of hearing it.

Every preacher is required to preach for 'verdict'. We are preaching under divine commission, and we don't have time to waste. Bishop Gore was addressing a group of young ordinands on the night before their ordination. He concluded his message with the words: 'Tomorrow I will say to you, "Will you, will you, will you?" . . . but one day another will ask, "Have you, have you, have you?"' As preachers we are exponents of the Good News and heralds of the new age, and we must always demand a response. One day we will be called to give account for what we have preached and how we preached it.

The call

Preaching will become relevant again as more and more young people hear the Lord's call to proclaim the word. They will speak it in new words, illustrate it in new ways and proclaim it with fresh vision.

Instead of saying, 'Sermons are boring,' I wish more young Christians would ask, 'Should I be preaching?' I'm thankful that older Christians encouraged me to test my call as a preacher when I was a teenager; and I'm grateful to those older preachers who nursed me through the early days of study and preparation.

I thank God for this calling, and try to remember Paul's words: 'For it is not ourselves that we preach; we preach Jesus Christ as Lord, and ourselves as your servants for Jesus' sake' (2 Cor 4:5).

The preacher

As I look back over my preaching ministry I sense that God has used me most effectively in three situations: when I've been scared, when I've been sick, and when I've been shattered. In other words, when I've reached the end of my own resources and cast myself upon the Lord. As I've come to Christ in desperate need of his help, I've known his blessing come.

Bishop Quayle summed it up when he wrote:

> The elemental business in preaching is not with the preaching, but with the preacher. It is no trouble to preach, but a vast trouble to construct a preacher. What then, in the light of this, is the task of the preacher? Mainly this, the amassing

of a great soul so as to have something worthwhile to give—the sermon is the preacher up to date.

WORKSHOP SESSION FIVE

Starter

The sermon clinic

Play a ten-minute audio tape or video tape of a sermon recorded from the radio or television. The whole group is asked to take notes during this sermon.

In groups of three discuss it together. Write a brief report from your discussion.

1. *Content* How did the preacher use the Bible? Did he make the points clearly, and did the message evoke a response in you?
2. *Presentation* Did the preacher speak clearly? Did he use his voice effectively? Was his style helpful—or did it distract from the message?
3. *General* Was the sermon well illustrated? Was it delivered with authority? Was it too long or too short? Did you understand it?

Share your reports together.

PS If a local preacher is willing, you could base this exercise around an actual Sunday sermon!

Activity

Preach it!

In groups of three, write a three-minute sermon! Each group must base their sermon around Luke 15:1–7. Remember to include material which illustrates your subject—and remember to speak for response.

Allow ten minutes for the group to write the sermons on the parable of the lost sheep. One person from each group 'preaches' the message.

Discuss together: How can congregations help preachers?

Question raiser

In pairs, look through the Bible and pick out verses, parables or sections which you would like to hear preached upon. Give each passage a title. List at least five readings and titles!

Share together the lists and collate them into a single list.

Submit this list to your local ministers or preachers and ask them to consider preaching on the passages listed.

Discuss together sermons that have influenced your lives.

Discussion questions

As a group, read these passages and talk about them together.

1. Ezekiel 33:30–32. List the wrong attitudes of the people.

2. Matthew 7:24–27. Why is preaching important?

3. Matthew 13:14–23. What kind of pressures take away and destroy the word we've received?

4. James 1:19–25. What kind of things about the word do you forget?

Closing prayers

Give each member of the group the name of a preacher who is scheduled to speak at your church in future months. Pray as a group for those who will come to preach and for those who preach regularly in your church.

6

Let Us Pray

The coach roared as it climbed up the steep hill beside the Sea of Galilee. Finally it reached the summit and turned into a lane beside the tree-lined church.

It was a quiet and beautiful place. My friends and I walked out on to the church veranda overlooking the Sea of Galilee. We stood and gazed at the beautiful scene, the rolling green hills reflected in the still blue waters of Galilee.

A thin mist in the distance lent an air of unreality to the scene. The stillness was tangible. Drifting from the church behind us came the muffled sound of singing. Time stood still.

After some minutes we began to pray with eyes wide open. Jesus seemed so close and prayer was natural and spontaneous. He was there and we shared our hearts with him. This was true prayer. Unassuming, personal, hushed, real; the kind of prayer he taught us to pray.

It was there on that hillside overlooking Galilee that Jesus said:

When you pray, do not use a lot of meaningless words, as the pagans do, who think that God will hear them because their prayers are long. Do not be like them. Your Father already knows what you need before you ask him. (Mt 6:7–8).

There were other lessons about prayer from our pilgrimage in Israel. We entered a lovely garden on the Mount of Olives, a white-walled place where Jesus taught his disciples to pray:

> Our Father which art in heaven,
> Hallowed be thy Name.
> Thy kingdom come,
> Thy will be done,
> In earth as it is in heaven.
> Give us this day our daily bread;
> And forgive us our trespasses,
> As we forgive them that trespass against us;
> And lead us not into temptation,
> But deliver us from evil.
> For thine is the kingdom,
> The power, and the glory
> For ever and ever. Amen (Prayer Book, from Mt 6:9–13).

We stood and watched the pilgrims from around the world praying the Lord's Prayer. It was quite challenging to realize that these simple phrases bound us to the people of every tribe and tongue.

Then our group gathered and recited the Lord's Prayer in English. It wasn't rushed or repeated with cold familiarity. We spoke each phrase with reverence and paused. Those oft-repeated words sounded new. I really meant each word I said. I was breathing fresh faith into familiar phrases.

I also learned about prayer in Gethsemane. We

walked down the hill past the tombs of countless generations and pushed open the gateway into the Garden. The
city traffic roared past beyond the garden wall. We made
our way into the quiet church; silence enveloped us. It
was a dark, shadowy place—reminiscent of that dark
night of betrayal. I found myself on my knees with the
scene of the garden filling my mind. I remembered: 'My
Father, if it is possible, take this cup of suffering from
me! Yet not what I want, but what you want' (Mt 26:39–
42).

A group of French pilgrims began to sing the words of
the Taizé chant 'Watch and Pray', a quiet sorrowful tune
with rich harmony. As I knelt there in the Garden
church I yielded my future to the will of the Father as
Jesus had done. This was prayer which demanded response. Heart, soul and mind yielded to the One I love.

My pilgrimage was soon over and the many beautiful
experiences of prayer filled my heart afresh. I only wish
that prayer in worship could be as meaningful as those
times in Israel. Unfortunately many of us find the times
of prayer in public worship very hard. The words 'Let us
pray' can be the signal to switch off. For many worshippers, corporate prayer has grown cold and mechanical.

It's so easy to criticize preachers for using self-
indulgent prayers, empty phrases said without thought
or preparation. It's so easy to criticize lay readers for
using prayers from books because they're cold and
formal. Perhaps, first of all, we should point the finger of
criticism at ourselves.

Many of us worshippers have lost the ability to 'practice the presence of God'. We have lost an awareness of
the Holy. We come to prayer with no desire to seek him,
and no hunger to meet the living God. We can turn out
new prayer books or train new preachers in leading corporate prayer, but our most urgent task must be to teach

congregations to pray with mind and spirit.

Corporate prayer demands full commitment of mind in concentration and of heart in faith. As Paul wrote: 'What should I do, then? I will pray with my spirit, but I will pray also with my mind' (1 Cor 14:15).

Prayer in church demands great effort from every worshipper. Too many of us are sitting back and expecting prayer to 'happen' without our input.

It isn't easy to love the Lord 'with all your mind' (Lk 10:27), particularly if your mind has a will of its own! We must learn how to capture and harness our thoughts and focus them in prayer. I'm personally aware of wandering thoughts during prayer in church. My mind is like a visual display unit charting priorities for the week ahead. Upcoming appointments to fulfil, phone calls to make and mail to answer! In focusing my mind in corporate prayer I have to turn each wandering thought into a prayer. I can then return to corporate prayer until the next wandering thought creeps in!

All kinds of things irritate me about the way in which prayers are led, and I really have to discipline myself to prevent my mind from 'switching off'. Some preachers gabble their prayers at such a rate that I just can't keep pace—I'm only on the first petition when they are on number five. I don't try to 'keep up', I just choose words and phrases and try to make them my own. Otherwise the whole thing becomes totally pointless.

Others launch into prayer without a pause for silence. They close their eyes and open their mouths to fill the silence with empty words. I have to spend a few seconds 'practising the presence of God' before I can pray. I must prepare myself, and if I miss the opening phrases I don't really worry.

Then there are prayers without specifics that irritate me too! We 'pray for Africa' or we 'pray for the poor'. I find it hard to exert faith for prayer as vague as this. I find myself turning such prayers into more manageable and specific requests.

Then there are depressing prayers! Long lists of the sad and the bad. Prayers that leave a cloud of despair over the worship. Prayers without hope! There is no explosion of believing faith within us and everyone feels depressed.

There are prayers which aren't prayers at all; camouflaged sermons, opinions paraded before the Almighty for approval, diatribes to which we're supposed to say 'Amen'. I find these prayers the hardest of all and sometimes feel obliged to turn away and pray alone.

Leading prayer in worship is an onerous task, and it's filled with dangerous possibilities. No wonder Jesus warned against the misuse of this kind of prayer when he said:

> When you pray, do not be like the hypocrites! They love to stand up and pray in the houses of worship and on the street corners, so that everyone will see them. I assure you, they have already been paid in full (Mt 6:5).

Every preacher must be warned against the dangers of parading his religion before others. But corporate prayer isn't all bad! Sometimes prayer in worship brings a special blessing. The one who leads the congregation can bring a freshness of faith to prayer that touches all our hearts.

I try to identify with the one who's leading us in prayer and to make his expressions mine. I try to summon my mustard seed of faith and add it to his words. I do my utmost to encourage him—even if it's only with a hearty 'Amen'! I try to remember that this is communication with the Lord. Prayer does change things, and its power far outweighs our understanding.

The book of Hebrews reminds us that prayer is futile without faith: 'To have faith is to be sure of the things we hope for, to be certain of the things we cannot see' (Heb 11:1). We don't need much—only a mustard seed's worth will do! But forms of words without the force of faith are meaningless indeed.

When the disciples couldn't drive out a demon from the young boy they couldn't understand what had gone wrong. 'It was because you haven't enough faith,' Jesus answered. 'I assure you that if you have faith as big as a mustard seed, you can say to this hill, "Go. . .".' (Mt 17:20).

In our congregational prayer we should aim to fill the prayers with faith. As a congregation we should add our 'mustard seeds' of faith together, so that miracles can happen.

Prayer should be the opportunity for this 'corporate release of faith'—not the chance for forty winks! It should lift us beyond the noise of children's voices, rustling sweet-wrappers, coughs and sneezes, to meet the living Saviour. We should know the reality of his presence and the joy of real communion with him.

> The Lord's unfailing love and mercy still continue, fresh as the morning, as sure as the sunrise. The Lord is all I have, and so I put my hope in him, (Lam 3:22–24).

Meaningful prayer

There are many ways of leading a congregation in prayer, but unfortunately very few of them are actually used. In many churches the forms of prayer have grown totally predictable. People seem to imagine that there is only one 'correct way' for a congregation to pray.

It would do some congregations good to rediscover *liturgical prayer*. They have used 'extempore prayer' for decades, and look down on prayers read from a book as if they were somehow 'inferior'. In so doing, they are despatching much of the church's great heritage of prayer to the scrap heap.

Some traditional written prayers mean a great deal to me. Recently it was my privilege to share in evensong at a local Anglican church. It was a long time since I'd taken part in read evensong, and I found it very comforting to come back to familiar words. It was like coming home. The poetry blessed me and I was really moved as the vicar said the words:

> God of peace who brought again from the dead our Lord Jesus Christ, that great shepherd of the sheep, by the blood of the eternal covenant: make us perfect in every good work to do your will, and work in us that which is well-pleasing in your sight; through Jesus Christ our Lord.

This kind of poetic style is rarely achieved with extempore prayer. While some preachers appear to be offering fresh prayers 'from the heart', they are in fact repeating oft-used phrases and worn-out expressions. Their prayers are as set as the strictest liturgy! Prayer in such churches could be refreshed by the use of prayer-books which have strengthened generations of our forefathers.

Other congregations might be encouraged to discover the use of *music* in prayer. Sung evensong is regularly held in many cathedrals and larger churches—it's a form of 'sung prayer'. There's no reason why prayer should only be sung in one musical style.

A good soloist or choir can lead a congregation in prayer to the very throne of God. Even folk or gospel music can be used to good effect, if we are willing to take the risk. As I was leading worship recently in a large theatre to the east of London, I invited the pianist to accompany my prayers of adoration and worship. The matching of theme was perfect, and we were drawn close to the Lord by this sensitive use of word and music.

Most of our churches in the United Kingdom have not discovered how to use *art* in prayer. This really came home to me when on holiday on a Greek island. On the Sunday morning my family and I made our way to the only church we could find, a Greek Orthodox cathedral. As the worship continued, people stood up and walked around freely.

All around the walls were pictures of Jesus. Many of the worshippers stood before these pictures—looking at them, praying, and kissing them. I'm aware of the danger of worshipping objects rather than the living God, but many of those people were using art as an inspiration for prayer.

In our art and banner-making workshops around the country, we have tried to encourage worshippers to discover the place of art in prayer. As groups have sewn and drawn and painted, they have paused to reflect and to pray.

The pictures and banners they have made have been brought into church for use during worship. Three kneeling figures before the risen Lord, and the words 'Where two or three are gathered'; the cross above a broken loaf, and the words "I am the bread of life"; a lighthouse spreading its beam far out to sea, and the words 'I am the light of the world.' We have used such pictures and symbols as a focus for prayer. We have invited the congregation to pause and look before they prayed. Sometimes we have encouraged them to pray with eyes wide open.

Sadly, many of our churches are devoid of art. Or their pictures are so old fashioned and unapproachable that they are useless for many worshippers. Frequently-changing displays, pictures and banners can be used as the inspiration for prayer. We can learn how to use these forms as a means and not an end.

Another kind of meaningful prayer can be seen in *healing services*. I admire the courage of a minister who has launched a series of these in a fairly traditional church. There need be nothing distasteful about such services and even the most sceptical can be convinced that they have a place.

My colleague generally holds such services in the context of Holy Communion. They are not 'loud' or 'emotional' but reverent and hushed acts of worship. After the last communicants have left the rail, the minister invites members of the congregation in special need to move forward for the laying on of hands. While the spiritual leaders of the church listen to each person's need, lay on hands and pray in faith, the rest of the congregation remain in silent prayer. Many have spoken of great blessing at such services.

There is ample biblical evidence that the laying on of hands during prayer was very much a part of the early church's life. Gifts of healing are given to the Body of Christ, and it is right and proper that we should meet in worship to claim them. We should launch out in specific prayer for those in need—with all the dangers inherent in this—for this is part of our life of faith.

The laying on of hands is a visual symbol of corporate faith. It's a demonstration of the power of communal prayer. It's a living example of loving fellowship. It's part of the church's corporate ministry of wholeness. We should incorporate it regularly into the church's worship life.

I thank God for those occasions when I have received the laying on of hands by friends who have gathered to ask God's blessing on my life. I am sure that this sort of thing is part of the church's ministry of prayer, and that the proper place for it is within worship.

Another aspect of prayer which many churches have lost is that of *confession*. The Bible says that we should not only confess our sins to God, but also to one another (Jas 5:16). Confession in many churches is over in a moment and barely appears in the liturgy. Congregational prayer should include enough space for admission of our failure, and this takes time.

It is too easy to confess our sins in one sweeping phrase. If we are to comprehend the reality of our sin we need to be specific. I have known members of a congregation stand and confess their sin, and there is a power and intensity in this which is quite wonderful.

At the very least there should be a space in every act of worship for the congregation to think back over previous days and to remember their sinfulness. Unless we honestly face up to the kind of lives we have been living we should not presume to ask for forgiveness.

It was the custom at many of Wesley's early Class Meetings for the people to confess their sins to each other every week and to encourage each other in a life of holiness. Our middle-class Christianity would not find this kind of thing very comfortable!

A few months ago I was sharing in a service for ministers in the north of England. The Holy Spirit descended on the meeting with such convicting power that the congregation was broken before the Lord. Many wept in repentance. If we all approached 'prayers of repentance' with heartfelt sorrow for the lives we have lived, perhaps they would lift off the page with new power and meaning.

Churches also need to discover the joy of *intercession*. As I sit in worship some Sundays these prayers seem designed to bore. They are a round-the-world trip taking in the latest famines, wars and disasters. The minister reels off a list of such morbidity that even the most joyous worshipper gets depressed!

Some ministers introduce their intercessions with a kind of morbid relish—'We've got a whole new set of disasters to pray about this week, folks.' After the final 'Amen' we open our eyes and look at each other. An air of depression fills the air, and the next hymn sounds like a funeral march.

I question if this is true intercession. It destroys faith rather than builds it. It breathes an atmosphere of negativism and gloom into people's hearts which is most destructive. Of course we live in an evil and cruel world, and we need to pray for it. But there are right ways and wrong ways of setting about it!

Over and over again in the Bible we see that the great leaders of faith placed their nation's needs within the context of God's almighty power. Prayer was an opportunity to get things in perspective, to remember God's resources; to channel their minds towards new beginnings, not bad endings!

Job himself had to learn this great lesson. He had to put the catalogue of disasters he had faced into the context of the love of God. In the end he was forced to admit: '[in the past] I knew only what others had told me, but now I have seen you with my own eyes. So I am ashamed of all I have said and repent in dust and ashes' (Job 42:5–6).

As God's people gather for prayer there should be an explosion of hope—not despair! We are committing all that hurts us most to One who stretches out to us with nail-pierced hands, and declares 'I am with you.'

Our churches also need to rediscover the joy of *meditation*. When I have visited monasteries, shared in retreats and talked to priests and nuns I have been very aware of my own lack of spirituality.

Many of us have never experienced the joy of meditation. We cannot focus our minds around a phrase of Scripture, a theme or a psalm for a few minutes, let alone a few hours!

Devotion doesn't come in pre-packed units. It comes through discipline, training and the sweat of the brow. We must invite people from other disciplines and denominations to share their experiences with us. Our worship should be enriched by the heritage of Christians far removed from us. Most adult congregations should be able to spend ten or fifteen minutes in guided meditation from time to time. There is a source of strength and joy in this which many of us have yet to discover.

There are many possibilities for a congregation of God's people which wants to pray! They can use music or art to focus their prayer. They can make repentance meaningful. They can focus their faith by laying on hands. They can make intercession joyful. They can pause for silent meditation.

When I was leading a time of prayer for about eighty ministers recently I became lost in wonder, love and praise. The sense of God's presence was so real that I lost track of time and the meeting over-ran. That's what prayer in worship should be like all the time! When a congregation approaches the living God in prayer they should be moving from the earthly to the heavenly. For. . .

> Our High Priest is not one who cannot feel sympathy for our weaknesses. On the contrary, we have a High Priest who was tempted in every way that we are, but did not sin. Let us be brave, then, and approach God's throne, where there is grace. There we will receive mercy and find grace to help us just when we need it. (Heb 4:15–16).

Styles of participation in prayer

I remember a long prayer-time one Sunday morning when the church was warm and I was very tired. As the preacher went on I began to doze off, but when the congregation said 'Amen' I was jolted awake. I just hoped that no-one noticed!

I sometimes wonder if I've sent people to sleep when I've led in prayer. I have a sneaking suspicion that people find themselves dozing peacefully during quite a lot of prayers. But there's one sure way of keeping everyone on their toes—we must get everyone involved!

I was leading worship in a huge suburban church. There were hundreds of people present, including Guides, Brownies, Scouts and Cubs. I knew as I looked at them that the prayer-time was just the excuse they were waiting for. There would be whispering, arm wrestling, and all manner of fun activities going on in the front pews while my eyes were closed!

So I produced a globe and talked about the greatness of the Lord who's got the whole world in his hands. Then I threw it at them to ensure they were awake! During the prayers of adoration I asked them to keep their eyes open and to use the globe as the focus for their prayers. There's nothing in the Bible that tells us we must always pray with our eyes shut!

During prayers of intercession I sometimes walk around the congregation inviting prayer requests. After each request I stop and pray out loud before moving on to the next. It's surprising what people will say if you give them the chance to share. It's important to give people some warning before this and to start by sharing something yourself. No one should be pressed to share a request if they don't want to. People should be given space to participate if they wish.

I have discovered that even young children are delighted to share a prayer request, and they long to let you know what's on their mind. They can write beautiful prayers which have a simple power about them. Children's art can also be used as an effective vehicle for prayers of adoration. If there are children present, they should be encouraged to participate fully in the prayer-time.

During our Creative Worship weekends we work with small groups in devising prayers for the worship. When we were on the Isle of Man some of the teenagers walked along the beach and collected sand, shells and seaweed. They brought it back and made a beautiful display on a table at the centre of our worship. They wrote 'Prayers from the seashore' which praised God for his greatness and power. On other weekends groups have gone into the country to get flowers and leaves and have used them to make prayers of adoration. It wasn't quite so easy for the group who used rubbish and debris from the city streets to construct a meditation on redemption!

There are many ways of involving people in prayers of intercession too: I sent three girls into Edinburgh one Saturday afternoon and commissioned them to write 'Prayers from a Wimpy Bar'. They structured the prayers around the people they met there and the kind of needs that were expressed. On our workshop weekends we often ask three people to write a prayer and another three to read it—so that six people within the congregation feel that they 'own' it.

Many churches use missionary prayer letters and newspapers as the source of information for prayer. It can be helpful to have specific information before us so that we can pray with real understanding.

Times of open prayer within an act of worship can be very uplifting, too, though there are a number of major snags to watch out for. It's often best if a microphone is used and that those wishing to lead come forward to pray—there's nothing worse than an inaudible mumble. It should also be made clear that short succinct prayers are needed, or the service could overrun!

The concept of everyone praying out loud at once may seem rather peculiar, but in many Pentecostal and West Indian churches this is quite a normal practice! It reminds them of the greatness of the God who can hear and answer all their prayers at once. This can be a way of encouraging people to pray out loud for the very first time, for no one will hear them except the Lord!

I also use 'Prayer scrummages'. The congregation divides up into groups of six or eight, and they put their arms around those beside them. The leader of each group invites people to share prayer requests and members of the group offer to pray for these either silently or out loud. Another way of involving people is by using a prayer request book. This is placed at the door before the service each week, and is brought forward for use by the preacher during the prayers of intercession.

Even if all of these other ideas seem totally unworkable, may I appeal to people to say 'Amen'? It makes such a difference if, at the end of a prayer, everyone else says AMEN—SO BE IT—WE AGREE!

WORKSHOP SESSION SIX

Starter

Newsround

Give each person several pages of a 'quality newspaper'. Use the latest edition available—there's nothing worse than 'old news'!

Each person spends a few minutes selecting one news story for prayer. Groups of three are formed, and they discuss their topics: Who are the important people in this story? What are the facts? What should we be praying for?

As a group, construct a short prayer of intercession about each news story. Each person should be prepared to read one of them.

Activity

Provide each person in the group with large sheets of paper, poster paints and brushes.

Provide a wallchart for the group on which are written these words:

> I am the light of the world. Whoever follows me will have the light of life and will never walk in darkness (Jn 8:12).

Everyone is asked to meditate on these words for a moment or two, and then to discuss their meaning with the person next to them.

Each person in the group is given five minutes to draw a picture or a symbol which communicates the meaning of the words for them. This is not an exercise to see who can draw the best picture—but an opportunity for each person to communicate what they feel.

Discuss the feelings behind your pictures rather than the pictures themselves. Put the pictures up around the walls.

Discussion questions

Each person needs a Bible. Look up Hebrews 11. Read verse 1 from several different translations.

Divide into groups of three. Each group is given one

'person of faith' from Hebrews to study, and is asked to read about this person in the Old Testament (e.g. for Abraham, described in Hebrews 11:17–19, the group would look up the cross-references in the Bible margin and read Genesis 22:1–14. It would be helpful to have a concordance or Bible dictionary available too.). Each group must tell the story of their faith-hero and explain how the story illustrates that faith is being sure of things hoped for.

Is faith important for prayer in worship?
Why?

Closing prayers

1. Use your pictures as a source of inspiration for prayers of praise and worship. The leader holds up each picture in turn and members of the group pray through its meaning. Everyone prays with eyes open.

2. Form a 'prayer scrummage' and intercede for the topics described in the newsround activity.

Remember to pray in faith!

7
The Power of the Spirit

Late one night the letterbox rattled, and the minister went to see what it was. There was no one there, just a pile of neatly addressed envelopes. He took them into his study and began to open them.

They were letters of resignation. From the church youth leaders. From the Sunday school teachers. From local preachers, and members of the church council. In a matter of minutes he had lost most of the young leaders of his three churches.

It was a devastating and painful blow. What had started as a group who were 'into renewal' had ended with a split in the fellowship. The nub of the issue was dissatisfaction with worship.

Some months later I became the minister of those churches, and I entered into some of the pain left by the split. Although I was in my first appointment as a minister, I quickly had to learn to encourage and build up those who were left.

It wasn't an easy task. The gap left by those young

leaders was very hard to fill. Finding new Sunday school teachers and youth leaders was nearly impossible, and battling against the prevailing atmosphere of gloom was a real challenge.

The split had not been as sweet or as clean as people had hoped. Lifelong friendships had ended. Some members of families had stayed, others had gone. There was an undercurrent of hurt and rejection among those who remained.

What disappointed me most was the suspicion about the renewal movement which lingered among the people who stayed. How could I blame them? They had seen the charismatic movement as the catalyst for division, and they wanted no more of it!

Every time I broached the subject of 'free worship', the 'use of the gifts', or the introduction of anything mildly 'charismatic' I could see many of the folk flinch. It just didn't seem the right time for such things.

At one time I hoped that I might be able to bring those who had left back into the fellowship. They knew that I was charismatic and shared their experience of the re-newing power of the Holy Spirit—but they wouldn't even consider returning to those traditional churches.

Who could blame them? They hired the local community centre, which was a light and modern building. They appointed their own elders, organized their own church life—and their fellowship prospered. They were able to use the gifts of the Holy Spirit freely in their worship every Sunday.

It is twelve years since this split occurred, and as I write this I have recently been driving through the area where it happened and remembering those early days of my ministry. The three Methodist chapels continue, although a good number of folk have come into an experience of renewal over the intervening years. The church in the community centre closed down long ago; its congregation has dispersed.

As I drove, I began to wonder if things could have worked out differently. Could those folk have worked through their misunderstandings? Could they have stayed together? And wouldn't the kingdom have been better served by unity?

This kind of heartache is going on nationwide. Wherever I go I hear stories of people leaving the established churches so that they can use the gifts of the Holy Spirit in worship. The kind of folk who are leaving are often young leaders, folk who are totally committed to Christ and long to see the kingdom come.

I can't believe that this trend is honouring to the Lord or helpful to the mission of the church. Yet I can understand what's causing it, because in my heart of hearts I've thought of leaving too. The attraction of being in fellowship with a large group of young families is really strong. The joy of worshipping with people who really know how to praise is great. The ordered but free use of the gifts of the Holy Spirit is something which I find both helpful and uplifting.

Compare that with the continued struggle of trying to please a congregation which has no sympathy with such things. Of holding yourself back in worship so that you embarrass no one. Of carrying a great weight of tradition which you find neither helpful nor meaningful. Of loving people who have no interest in your new experience nor desire to share it.

No wonder that many ministers have grown wary of the charismatic movement. They see it as a potential force for division. No wonder that many congregations have silently decided that they want none of this 're-newal'; they are afraid that it will bring changes they are neither willing nor able to contemplate.

Where then is the answer to this seemingly impossible conundrum? I believe it is to be found in theology! For although 'renewed' and 'traditional' Christians may share different experiences of worship and church practice, we should all share together the same doctrine of the Holy Spirit!

Perhaps it is time for many faithful 'traditional' churchgoers to look again at the person of the Holy Spirit. Maybe this is the key to fresh worship, church renewal and personal growth. Maybe some of my arm-waving, tongue-speaking charismatic friends need to look again at the doctrine and work of the Holy Spirit. All the trappings of 'renewed' worship are nothing if they are not based on a firm understanding of who the Holy Spirit is.

It is quite impossible to look at worship without looking at the person and work of the Holy Spirit. But I sense that this is one of the most painful and contentious areas of worship renewal, and I write out of a deep desire for unity and not division. There are three aspects of the work of the Holy Spirit which I hope will unite us all.

1. Power

Some years ago we toured the United States with our Gospel Roadshow. Eventually our tour took us to Niagara Falls; it was a tremendous experience. I was fascinated by the beauty and power of the magnificent waterfall.

One of the many tourist trips available at the Falls was a chance to go into the caverns behind Niagara. The guide gave us waterproofs, and then led us down dark passageways behind the huge waterfall. Eventually we reached a cavern and were able to look out through an opening toward daylight. The scene was indescribable.

We were actually standing behind the huge torrent of water. The roar was deafening. Rainbows danced in the spray, and we got soaked!

The guide explained that there were plans to build a hydro-electric turbine in the cave and to 'turn off' the Falls at night. The water would plunge through the turbine and create enough energy to light many of the Northern States of America.

I found this idea mind-blowing. This one waterfall had the power to drive hundreds of factories and to light millions of homes. Only the Americans could dream up such a huge project! But then I thought of the power of God, the Holy Spirit. The power which holds the stars in space. The power which holds the earth in orbit and brings the seasons in their turn. This is the power without limit, the power of God.

The same power which moved over the waters at creation is available today. The power which brought order out of chaos is God's gift to the church. The power which brought the glory of creation out of the void can move among us now. This is the power for new worship!

Yet much of our worship seems to deny this power. It is safer to stick to familiar ways and well-known paths! There is something very disturbing and unpredictable about asking for the power of the Holy Spirit to renew our worship.

Some of us are guilty of quenching the power of the Holy Spirit; as Paul wrote to Timothy, 'they hold to the outward form of our religion, but reject its real power.' (2 Tim 3:5). There is no excuse for this.

The central question for all who want to see worship changed must be: 'Do we want our worship to be under the anointing of the Holy Spirit?' If we do, we need to set time apart in our busy church schedules to identify this need and to seek the living God. I long that all congregations would gather to pray for the renewing power of the Holy Spirit.

Here then is common ground between those who are charismatic and those who aren't. We should be united in a common prayer that God will send the Holy Spirit to renew every aspect of our worship. Even more important than worship workshops, discussions over liturgy or the exploration of new forms, should be the prayer

> Spirit of the living God, fall afresh on me!
> Break me, melt me, mould me, fill me,
> Spirit of the living God, fall afresh on me.

2. Availability

There is a park near my home where I love to go to pray and meditate. I often walk beside a small bubbling stream, and I love the sound of the water on the pebbles. It's a quiet tranquil place, and I often sense the presence of the Lord there.

As I was walking through the park one day I noticed that a water board official had closed the floodgates, and the stream was shut off. All that remained was a muddy channel. Flies hovered over it and it stank. I didn't stay long that day! It was all dried up. The picture of that dried-up stream spoke to me about my life, and the way that I often felt 'dried up' spiritually. I began to realize that this wasn't the Lord's best way for me.

I had been looking on the power of the Holy Spirit as a watering-hole—and not as a stream! I had imagined that I had to go to special meetings, conventions or rallies to get 'topped up' with the Holy Spirit so that I could journey on through the wilderness. I had become a kind of evangelical camel!

I realized afresh that the Holy Spirit is a never-ending

stream welling up within each of us. Jesus said to the woman at the well, 'The water that I will give him will become in him a spring which will provide him with life-giving water and give him eternal life!' (Jn 4:14). We need not go through 'dried up' times because the stream of the Holy Spirit is always within us—always filling us.

Some feel that the Holy Spirit only moves after they have sung a set number of choruses. Or that the Holy Spirit only comes if they hold up their arms, or are led by a suitably recommended worship leader. Or, even more dangerous, that the Holy Spirit only moves among their denomination or within their grouping.

That is rubbish! The diversity of activity of the Holy Spirit is far greater than we can ever understand. When Jesus said, 'But I am telling you the truth: it is better for you that I go away, because if I do not go, the Helper will not come to you. But if I do go away, then I will send him to you' (Jn 16:7)—he really meant it!

The prerequisites of the coming of the Holy Spirit upon us are basic indeed. Repentance; forgiveness of sins by the sacrificial death of Jesus; salvation; and a thirst for the Lord's renewing power, his gift to the church!

The Holy Spirit's renewing power is available to all Christian churches. No one group or denomination has a monopoly on the working of the Holy Spirit. Your local church or fellowship—no matter how small and weak—has a rightful claim on the 'Helper', the power of the Holy Spirit.

It is this simple concept which has kept me within Methodism in some of the darkest patches of my ministry. I have believed with all my heart that the Holy Spirit was available for me, and for the churches I have served, without having to go elsewhere to find him. If only some of my charismatic friends would take seriously the availability of the Holy Spirit, they might stay longer in their local church. Sadly, many have left because they say they 'find the Spirit' elsewhere.

The Holy Spirit is available to you and to your church. The question is, are you willing to receive him there?

3. Unity

Recently my wife and I and our two sons Andrew and Christopher went for a long walk in the country. We came across a lovely brook with a small wooden bridge across it.

We stood on the bridge with twigs in our hands, and at the word 'go' let them drop into the water. We then raced along beside the stream to see whose twig would round the bend first. It was great fun, and the force of the water was such that the twigs moved really quickly. We would have been more than surprised if one of the twigs had moved against the flow, and motored upstream back to the bridge.

In the river of the Spirit, there is a current which should bring unity. All believers should be moving in the same direction under the gentle flow of the Holy Spirit. Paul exhorted the Ephesians in this way by saying:

> Be always humble, gentle and patient. Show your love by being tolerant with one another. Do your best to preserve the unity which the Spirit gives by means of the peace that binds you together. There is one body and one Spirit, just as there is one hope to which God has called you' (Eph 4:2–4).

I think it's very sad that experiences of charismatic renewal in many churches over recent years have been divisive. Often the folk in one house group or one peer group grow away from the rest of the congregation.

Time and again in the Bible, we read that there is a

corporate nature to the renewing power of the Holy Spirit. On the day of Pentecost the early church was gathered together and were *all* filled with the Holy Spirit. (Cf. Acts 2:1). When Peter and John returned from their appearance before the Council they met with the others and prayed for boldness. The Bible says that 'When they finished praying, the place where they were meeting was shaken. They were *all* filled with the Holy Spirit and began to proclaim God's message with boldness' (Acts 4:31, my italics). In Joppa it was not only Cornelius who received the Spirit but 'the Holy Spirit came down on *all* those who were listening to his message' (Acts 10:44, my italics).

The story of the Lord's work at Greenhill Methodist Church in Sheffield is quite widely known. In May 1981, on a Sunday morning, the minister and about seventy members walked out to form a new church. Soon afterwards the remaining members met together to seek God's will and to plan their future life together. Over the last few years the renewal of worship has gradually developed. The minister, the Rev. John Trevenna, writes in *Dunamis* magazine (a mainly Methodist renewal quarterly):

> The worship has become a living reality—not by 'forcing' choruses, or tongues, but by allowing God's Spirit to be free—to clap or not to clap, to raise hands or not to raise hands, to sing a chorus twice, or not to sing it at all!!!

When asked 'How would you describe Greenhill church now?' Mr Trevenna replied:

> It is a united church, there is no division, but it is NOT that we are united by an overtly Charismatic emphasis, we are united by the LOVE of Jesus and isn't that what it's all about?

This is the key to uniting a church which is 'partly

renewed' in the Holy Spirit. We should not try to find or force a unity based on 'charismatic' experience; our unity should be based in the person of Jesus Christ.

It's really sad that in some churches the power of the Holy Spirit has seemed to divide rather than unite. When the Holy Spirit renews us we should have an even greater capacity for caring about the Unity of the Body than before. One of my friends used to say that the coming of the Holy Spirit is like the two wings of a bird. The gifts are one wing, and the fruit are the other. You can have all the gifts, or all the fruit—but you'll not 'lift off' without both!

And the fruit of the Spirit is: 'love, joy, peace, patience, kindness, goodness, faithfulness, humility, and self-control' (Gal 5:22–23). We need churches rich in gifts, and bearing much fruit!

Power in worship

Most Christians could accept that the Holy Spirit is powerful, that he is available to us all, and that his coming should unite us. The problems really start when the Holy Spirit leads a congregation into forms of worship which some find disturbing—or even distasteful. It is here that I must own up to the fact that I am a reluctant charismatic, and that in many ways I share great sympathy with those who find the renewal movement quite unmanageable!

I first heard about the renewal of the Holy Spirit when I was a student at Cliff College. I had been a committed Christian for some years, and all this talk about the 'Pentecostal' experience was all very new to me. Someone persuaded me to go to a Pentecostal prayer meeting one night, and I went out of curiosity. I found the whole thing quite horrific. Speaking in tongues, casting out of demons and words of 'knowledge' were not a part of my Methodist heritage (or so I thought!).

It was some months later that we held a 'quiet day' at the college, a day for silent meditation and reflection. I found it quite a strain because I am a natural 'talker'. But during the afternoon of the quiet day I settled down to further study of the power of the Holy Spirit, and concluded that I needed to know this source of renewing power in my life.

I lay prostrate on the floor of my college room and wept over my sin. I pleaded with the Lord to fill me with the power of the Holy Spirit so that I could be a 'channel of blessing'. Without being present at a great meeting and without having hands laid on my head I knew that God had filled me, and I began to speak in strange tongues.

It was like a new door opening for me. Where my own earthly language ran out, I had found a new way of expressing my love and devotion for the Lord. What I had considered distasteful and outrageous a few months earlier was now my treasured experience. Very often in worship I speak quietly to the Lord in tongues. In charismatic gatherings I love to join the whole fellowship in singing or speaking in tongues.

Having made my first reluctant steps into charismatic worship I have gradually grown in confidence and assurance. But new charismatic experiences have generally come because I've been thrown in at the deep end. For example, after one Pentecostal rally I found myself with other elders laying hands on the sick. Quite wonderful things happened as a result, and I can only rest assured that it wasn't anything to do with me!

As I have become more accustomed to charismatic worship I have found the orderly use of spiritual gifts to be an inspiring part of worship. At meetings where beautiful visions and prophecies have been shared there has been a real sense of God communicating with his people.

And on two occasions in recent months I have been called upon to exercise a ministry of deliverance. Not by choice, you understand, but because I seemed the only person around at the time who was willing to take authority over the power of evil. Here was I, the reluctant charismatic, in at the deep end!

Members of my team have been empowered on certain occasions to share spontaneous dance, word, and music. The sense of hushed awe which has followed such occurrences has been a sign of the Spirit's presence. Paul said:

> The Spirit's presence is shown in some way in each person for the good of all. The Spirit gives one person a message full of wisdom, while to another person the same Spirit gives a message full of knowledge. One and the same Spirit gives faith to one person, while to another person he gives the power to heal. The Spirit gives one person the power to work miracles; to another, the gift of speaking God's message; and to yet another, the ability to tell the difference between gifts that come from the Spirit and those that do not. To one person he gives the ability to speak in strange tongues, and to another he gives the ability to explain what is said. But it is one and the same Spirit who does all this; as he wishes, he gives a different gift to each person (1 Cor 12:7–11).

Paul's list reveals the rich diversity of gifts which the Holy Spirit can bring to our worship life. Such gifts are given to bring glory to Jesus Christ and to encourage and build up the church. They are not to be thought of lightly. The gifts of the Holy Spirit are shrouded in mystery.

I entered the large London Anglican church with some

degree of apprehension. I'd heard that it was a charismatic church, but I'd never been handed a prayer book on my way into a 'charismatic service' before! The church was full for this ordinary Sunday evening service. Hundreds of young people were present, both black and white. The sense of anticipation among those who gathered was very beautiful.

The read order of Holy Communion was interspersed with lively modern worship songs led by an excellent music group. The sermon was biblical and challenging, and the joy of worship was real. The sacrament of Holy Communion was followed by a time of open ministry. There were those who spoke in tongues—and there was interpretation. These words brought both challenge and encouragement to the local folk.

People in need gathered quietly for the laying on of hands for healing or for deliverance. All was done reverently, and in order, with a great sense of Christ's presence as the focus of it all. Many returned from this time of ministry with a new joy and peace shining from their faces.

Here was a wonderful mix of worship styles. The traditional and the contemporary; the liturgical and the free; the noisy and the quiet; the orthodox and the charismatic. I returned home full of thanksgiving for what I'd seen and shared.

The gifts of the Holy Spirit are given for the enrichment of contemporary worship. Even in the most traditional of churches there is no reason why we should not give space for some charismatic aspects of worship.

Yet we must all share Paul's great concern for order. There is nothing more dishonouring in worship than a total mess! Whatever is done should be ordered, and given for God's glory alone. Paul warned:

If someone is going to speak in strange tongues, two or three at the most should speak, one after the other, and someone else must explain what is being said. But if no one is there who can explain, then the one who speaks in strange tongues must be quiet and speak only to himself and to God (1 Cor 14:27–28).

As we gather to worship the Lord, we need the renewing power of the Holy Spirit to help us. The Spirit may come as we sing our traditional hymns or say our familiar liturgies. He may come through prophecies, inspired words and tongues. He may come in the silence.

Whether we come from the 'charismatic' stable or the 'traditionalist' lobby we share much in common. All of us need to learn more of the work of the Holy Spirit, and how he is active in worship. All of us need to pray for personal renewal in the Holy Spirit, and for the renewing of the churches to which we belong.

No matter how hopeless we may feel about our local church worship, it's a great comfort to know that the power of the Holy Spirit is there to help us! Paul wrote:

In the same way the Spirit also comes to help us, weak as we are. For we do not know how we ought to pray; the Spirit himself pleads with God for us in groans that words cannot express. And God, who sees into our hearts, knows what the thought of the Spirit is; because the Spirit pleads with God on behalf of his people and in accordance with his will (Rom 8:26–27).

WORKSHOP SESSION SEVEN

Starter

This is a light-hearted activity to get people relaxed!
Give everyone a small piece of paper. They are asked

to make a 'wind-efficient sail'.

Then each person is given a drinking straw. They have to propel their 'sail' along a shiny table, by blowing through the straw.

See whose sail goes furthest!

In John 3 and Acts 2 the Holy Spirit is described as a strong wind.

Why?

Slogans

Divide into groups of three.

Each group has a Bible concordance, and looks up the section of references marked 'Holy Spirit'.

The group must read through a selection of passages and construct a number of slogans to be painted on church walls.

Each group must create at least three slogans to be painted on the interior walls for the congregation, and three slogans to be painted on the outside walls for the benefit of passers by.

Discuss: If the power of the Holy Spirit descended on us—as at Pentecost—what difference would it make to our life in the church and our life in the world?

Study

Read Acts 4:12–16.

What kind of miracles were apparent in the early church? Each group makes a list.

Should 'signs and wonders' be a part of normal church life today? Could they become part of your local church life?

If not—why not?

Closing prayers

In groups of three, list six members of the congregation not present at the meeting. Pray for these six people, that the Lord will bless them in their work and witness within the local church.

Get back together as a whole group. Pray for the leadership of your church and for your common life. Thank God for each other—and ask for the renewing power of the Holy Spirit on your worship.

8

Broken Church

The pain

I thought that my family services were rather good. My youth leaders didn't. After family service one day they came to protest. They threatened to withdraw the uniformed organizations from worship unless the services improved.

We had a meeting about it, and I took their comments seriously. The changes weren't too startling. I shortened everything, included more participation, simplified my approach, and generally made the atmosphere more relaxed. The children responded well, and the leaders were delighted. Right after the 'new format' family service they came to show their appreciation. I felt really good about the whole thing.

Just after they'd gone, I was cornered by a smartly dressed lady who had attended the church for years. 'That service was dreadful,' she protested. 'If there's ever another like it I'll resign my membership.'

I went home and made myself a strong cup of coffee. I sat slumped in the chair and protested to my wife, 'I can't win; I please one group in the church and I offend another!'

At about the same time I had real problems with our youth group. They were a great bunch of teenagers, and many of them were new Christians. Every Sunday evening they would come to church and sit in the front row! It looked quite odd, because nearly everyone else sat at the back. One Sunday evening, just as I was about to launch into a sermon of which I was particularly proud—the whole group stood up and walked out! It was most off-putting, and I found it hard to continue.

Afterwards, at the youth fellowship, I asked them why. They told me that they found my sermons boring, so they'd decided to leave at that point in the service to get the coffee ready! This didn't do my ego much good, so I challenged them to do better themselves.

We began going round the circuit and taking services as a group. We discussed the theme at youth fellowship, and then they prepared drama, testimony, and song for the following week's service. One dark November night they led a very beautiful service in a poorly attended South London church. I was really encouraged, and I told them so. My joy soon turned to pain when a man at the door told me it was the worst service he'd known in sixty years of churchgoing!

Broken church

When I began to travel about the country I discovered that the pain I was experiencing in my own ministry was nothing unusual. The pain of ministers and youth leaders, who are often at the front line of this kind of problem, has to be seen to be believed. In our 'Young

People and Worship' consultations we have discussed these problems with over 1,500 youth leaders and ministers. The heartache is nationwide.

One minister shared with great emotion the hatred he had encountered when making minor changes with worship. Members of his congregation got up a petition to have 'services the way they used to be.' Older people in the village were asked to sign the petition before collecting their pensions from the post office counter.

A youth group who had discovered the joy of expressing their faith in drama asked for the choir pews to be replaced with movable seating, so that there could be space for their input. The church council agreed, but the criticism from others in the church was so great that the proposal had to be dropped.

Our role-plays of church councils have often led to times of deep sharing. Ministers have confessed the pain of trying to hold different factions together in worship. Youth leaders have described the dissatisfaction felt by their young people with the dullness and traditionalism of most church worship.

The tension

I have gone out of my way in the last few years to try to identify what the tensions over worship are. In role-play I have sometimes taken the part of the traditionalist, and tried to get inside the feelings of those people who want things to stay the same. In doing so, I have come to understand that for many people, worship is like an island of security in a changing world. The familiar hymns and unchanging liturgies touch on memories and experiences which are at the core of faith.

Drama, modern music and the creative arts appear to be an invasion into their approach to God. Participation seems threatening, and changes disturb the tranquil pool of quiet at the end of a busy week. Changes to the building seem sacrilegious. Plastic seating and neon lights do not mix easily with thoughts of the Eternal. Here is a place where change is barred, for this is where time stands still.

As I've listened to teenagers talking about worship I have been alarmed at what I've heard. Our culture has changed so fast and so far in the last fifty years that many young people entering worship for the first time feel they're in a time warp. The building and the forms of worship we use are foreign to the light, life and colour of contemporary pop culture. The idea of sitting still for an hour or more is something which many young people haven't experienced at school. They're used to participation.

But until people from different cultures in church life start listening to each other and attempting to understand each other, there's no chance of change without division. The older statesmen of church life need to start hearing what young people are saying and vice-versa.

The occasional 'youth service' is not a realistic response to this problem. It is patronizing. It only makes the divisions sharper. The young people have to put up with the old form for the next fifty-one Sundays. They have had no more than a glimpse of what worship could become.

'The Body of Christ'

The Christians in early church life faced many tensions, too. The church in Corinth, for example, was torn apart by division. The city itself was a mixture of many different religious ideas. Corinth was politically Roman and socially Greek, but in terms of religion it was Roman,

Greek and Oriental all rolled into one! And the Corinthian church felt the tensions of the cosmopolitan society in which it was placed. It had members like Crispus and Sosthenes who viewed everything through Jewish eyes, because they were also rulers of the synagogue. Yet it also contained many Gentiles. There were rich people like Gaius, and powerful people like the city treasurer, Erastus. But there were also slaves, Jewish refugees and former thugs within the membership.

This young church was near to collapse because of the diversity of ideas its members held. There was dreadful immorality among the membership and disorder in the church meetings. Christians were even taking each other to court. If we think we've got problems in our modern church life, we haven't begun to realize what problems the Corinthian church was facing!

It was into this conflict and disarray that Paul wrote his allegory of the church as the 'Body of Christ'. It must have had a powerful impact on those who received it! Paul stressed that no part of the body could feel superior or inferior to another.

It's a lesson which many of our contemporary congregations need to learn! The charismatics are not superior to the traditionalists. Nor are those who prefer a 'formal liturgy' superior to those who opt for 'free worship'. The foot is as much a part of the body as the hand, and the ear as the eye. There is a deep sense of interdependency in every bodily part. Chrysostom the early church father wrote, 'The head is crowned and all the members have a share in the honour, the eyes laugh when the mouth speaks.'

Paul's allegory of the body speaks to our situation very clearly. The diversity of the different parts of the body are its strength. This is what makes the body work! The ear does one job, and the eye another; but they both need each other. The insights and preferences of different groups within church life should complement each other and not bring division.

If only we could grasp Paul's message, our churches would be more whole. Worship would be enriched by our diversity of tastes and ideas and not destroyed by them. Our different gifts in worship would operate in unison under the rule of Christ, the head of the body.

When hearing conflicting opinions about worship, I've wanted to bring all parties together and declare 'You are the Body of Christ . . . can the hand say to the foot "I don't need you?"' (Cf. 1 Cor 12:12–26).

One of the church's most urgent tasks is to develop a worship life which crosses all cultures and unifies its people in love and praise. If there are different pressure groups within the worship life of a local church, it is clear that we have not discovered either the pain, or the joy, of being the Body of Christ: the community of God's people.

Starting where the people are at

I have recently been challenged to stop and examine my motives for worship renewal. In his book entitled *Worship as Pastoral Care*, William H. Willimon asks some helpful questions:

> In reaching for that something more in worship, we approach our best motives for a pastoral concern for worship. The question before us is not: Shall I innovate in worship? Shall we have more spontaneity or more formality? The most appropriate questions are: In what ways can I as a pastor help my congregation to worship? . . . Edification, upbuilding, is our chief pastoral goal.

I know from my own ministry that I have sometimes

pushed for changes that in hindsight have been intended more to fulfil my own needs than those of the local worshipping community.

If there is to be a deepening of the worship life of a local congregation we have to start where people are, not where we'd like them to be. One group can move so fast in changing worship that the rest of the congregation feel unable to relate to what is going on. They switch off and become alienated. They can no longer understand the pattern of worship, and they become embittered because the familiar has been taken away.

People who prefer more traditional forms have a lot to teach us, and I've begun to recognize the fact. In my 'angry' youth I would have scorned much of what we call 'traditional' worship. But now I'm not so sure. Sir John Betjeman spoke for many when he wrote:

> All I can say is that with age I find myself enjoying more and more the words and rhythms of the Book of Common Prayer. Apart from their meaning, they sound right and they are not talking down to us by being matey, and where they're a bit vague and archaic, that makes them grand and historic. The words give me time to meditate and pray; they are so familiar, they are like my birthplace, and I don't want them pulled down.

When I was preaching in a small Cotswold town I spoke to a number of older Methodists who had seen their young people desert the 'chapel' for the nearby 'house church'. It had obviously left a very great deal of hurt. There had been many causes for the split, but the most contentious related to the pattern and style of Sunday worship.

I was amused when at breakfast time the following morning I met a young leader from the house church who called in to see me. We talked for some time about the 'split' and how the new house church was developing. Just before he left he said, 'You'll never guess what happened at our house church last Sunday! We discovered Wesley's hymns. Aren't they great?'

There was, after all, something from traditional worship which had value and importance! I only regretted that they'd had to leave Methodism to discover the great pearl of Methodist worship tradition! Many who have written off all 'traditional worship' need to think again.

Work at 'community'

People often ask my advice about 'dead worship'. They are generally contemplating one of two quick-fire solutions. The first is that they leave the church, and find another more suited to their taste in worship. This may sometimes be necessary, though it is always very sad. I try to encourage such people to see that, as part of the Body, they have a duty and obligation to stay and contribute the gifts the Lord has given them. For without their input the 'local Body' will be robbed of insights which it probably needs.

The second is that they propose a manifesto of new ideas that they intend to railroad through the committees of the church, so that their worship can be quickly brought to life. In my experience such rapid changes bring nothing but division and alienation. Worship can't be renewed in a day or even a decade. We're talking of long-term investment in a local church or congregation.

The churches which seem to have developed their worship life fastest have made their first priority prayer, and their second the strengthening of the church's community life together. Worship is essentially the outward expression of a church's life as a community.

The more that people gather informally midweek, the

more real will be their offering of worship as a community of God's people on a Sunday. Sadly, much of our church life segregates the old from the young, the children from the over-sixties. Often people from other peer groups can seem a threat to our age and interest group.

One small town church on the Welsh borders was having real difficulty over the changing of worship styles. The youth leader was sensitive to the growing tension and felt that bridges needed to be built between the old and the young. The youth group started serving coffee after worship each Sunday morning, and were briefed to stop and talk at each table as they served the drinks. It was only a small gesture, but it was an important beginning. It began to cut away the feeling of 'us' and 'them' which had built up between the teenagers and the older people in the church.

In the same way, churches that go on holiday together, that hike together, that picnic together and that share bonds of friendship across the generations are churches that are more likely to move forward with unity.

It isn't always older people who are most critical of changes in worship styles. Sometimes older folk are the most enthusiastic about change. Young people may be the ones who most want things to stay the same! But wherever the tensions are, the first priority must be to get people befriending each other, getting to know one another, and starting to hear what each other are saying. Some people need to learn about the joy and liberation which can be found in new forms. Others need to learn why some traditional aspects of worship can bring great blessing.

One thing's for sure. Where congregations broken apart by division and bitterness try to worship, God is not honoured. Jesus said:

So if you are about to offer your gift to God at the altar and there you remember that your brother has something against you, leave your gift there in front of the altar, go at once and make peace with your brother, and then come back and offer your gift to God (Mt 5:23–24).

Some of us need to learn patience, and grace. And some of us need to leave our gift in front of the altar and go to make peace with our brethren.

WORKSHOP SESSION EIGHT

Starter

Divide into groups of three. Two people are excluded from this exercise. These two must leave the room.

Each group must devise as many ways of giving someone 'the cold shoulder' as possible: e.g. body language, terms of phrase, disinterest, being engrossed in another conversation.

The two strangers then enter and move individually from group to group trying to make friends and join in conversation.

After they have visited every group, discuss how the groups felt, and how the strangers felt.

Discuss: Could this possibly happen at your church?
How can you improve the depth of fellowship and caring?

Activity

Members of the group form an imaginary church council. Give the church a name—and stress it is not your local church! Think carefully before allocating parts within the group.

The minister: The minister is fresh out of college. He has no experience. This is the first meeting the minister has chaired. This character comes over as very shy, and very nervous. He tends to agree with everyone, in order to keep the church together!

The secretary: The secretary of the meeting was given the job while he was on holiday. He had no interest in it. He is extremely deaf, always misunderstanding what has been said, and also wants to get home quickly to watch a favourite programme on TV—so hurries the meeting along by constantly suggesting that the committee moves to the next business.

The traditionalist: This eighty-six year old was present at the church stone-laying eighty-five years ago! He longs to get back to the good old days when the church was full and the congregation sang gospel hymns; likes quiet meditation and well-known liturgy, and an opportunity to enjoy familiar forms of worship; feels threatened by change. This part should be played by someone under twenty-five years of age!

The traditionalist's friend: This seventy-six year old plays dominoes with the Traditionalist in the 'over-sixties'. They are close friends. This person supports all that the traditionalist says, and gets very angry when the Young Trendy speaks! He may even become violent; and if provoked, may resign his seat on the church council and storm out.

The young trendy: This twenty-three year old wants to see worship revolutionized. The pews should be pulled out, loudspeakers should replace the pulpit. Coke and crisps should be served at communion. Reggae music and chart-topping songs should be used to pinpoint themes. This character is rather 'over the top', wears outlandish style clothes and spiky hair, is very aggressive, and tends to alienate everyone else on the committee! Should be played by someone over sixty years old.

The Christian teenager: This shy young Christian is making a first appearance at the church council. Says hardly anything, and when she tries is quickly smothered by the others. Everyone wants her vote, but no one is interested in her opinion. By the end of the meeting she is close to tears.

The irritant: This person just goes on and on about another church she's visited. Has no idea why this church is so wonderful—but goes on telling everyone that their church is hopeless by comparison. Has the effect of making everyone feel totally inadequate. Perhaps they should close down and join the other church?

The pious person This person is slightly too heavenly minded to be any earthly good! The result is that she keeps asking everyone to pray. This 'heavenly minded' approach annoys everyone else.

The role-play begins when the minister says

'How can we involve the young people in our worship:'

Allow it to run for between five and ten minutes. Don't worry if the action is slow at first—it usually gets quite heated!

The members of the role-play should be seated in a circle, with the rest of the group around them.

Question raiser

Ask each person to remain in their seat in the circle. One by one, the characters in the role play are invited to talk about the people they were portraying.

What makes people talk like that?
What was happening in the group?

Did people listen to the others?
What kind of fears were being expressed?
How did the minister feel?

The wider group is then invited to discuss:
In which ways can we see reflections of our own church in this role-play?
Do we really listen to each other in our fellowship?
If not—why not?

Discussion questions

Read together 1 Corinthians 12:12–31.

1. 'In the same way, all of us, whether Jews or Gentiles, whether slaves or free, have been baptized into the one body by the same Spirit' (v.13)

What does Paul mean by 'baptized into the one body by the same Spirit?'

How do you think the following felt when they heard this?

    a. Gentiles.
    b. slaves.
    c. free.
    d. Jews.

2. 'For the body itself is not made up of only one part, but of many parts' (v.14).

Is diversity within the church a strength, or a weakness?

3. 'So then, the eye cannot say to the hand, "I don't need you!" Nor can the head say to the feet, "Well, I don't need you"' (v.21).

In which ways do people say 'I don't need you' to others in the Body of Christ today?

4. 'So there is no division in the body, but all its different parts have the same concern for one another' (v.25).

How can you tell a church which is really putting this into practice?

5. 'All of you are Christ's body, and each one is a part of it' (v.27).

How can a church develop a congregational life in which the people are operating like a body?

Closing prayers

If appropriate, sing some songs about Christian fellowship.

Each person in the group is asked to make a suggestion as to how the local church can be more united.

Each person in the group then turns their suggestion into a prayer.

Hold hands and say the grace to each other.

9

The Influence of Culture

The Land Rover stopped. The rough track had ended and I was to continue my journey on foot. Walking along the wooded path that humid Kenyan afternoon was exhausting, and by the time I arrived at the church I was really tired.

It was quite the strangest church I'd ever seen. There was no building, just a sprawling tree in the centre of a clearing. A large sign listed the times of services, and the worshippers gathered beneath its spreading branches.

Soon the clearing was full of people. They sang and swayed and praised the day away. There were no hymn books; just songs improvised as the Spirit led. There was no pipe organ; just the beat of drums. There was no seating; just plenty of room for dance and movement. This was authentic African worship and I loved every minute of it.

There, beneath the tree, the Kenyan Christians were worshipping the Lord in ways appropriate to their culture. Ancient dances took on new meanings. Old harmonies carried new words. Traditional songs were adapted to praise God's name. Christian worship was being expressed in genuine Kenyan culture.

Not many miles away I joined another Kenyan congregation for worship. They sang English hymns, read English prayers, and struggled to sing English tunes unsuited to African harmony. There was a pipe organ, a brick building and a church bell. I might as well have stayed at home.

This was an example of culture-bound worship. Someone somewhere had failed to understand that there are more ways to praise the Lord than in stereotyped English liturgies. They had forced African worship into an English mould.

It's easy to assume that 'our way of worship is the only way'. How bigoted we are! The Lord does not enjoy only our kind of singing or appreciate only our style of praying, and he doesn't despise what others wish to offer. I fear that many of us force our preferences on to those from different cultures who would naturally worship in different ways.

The woman of Samaria asked Jesus if God should be worshipped at the holy place in Samaria or in Jerusalem. She wanted to know if 'Samaritan culture' worship was as acceptable to the Lord as 'Jerusalem-style' worship. Jesus made it clear that location was irrelevant.

> The time is coming and is already here, when by the power of God's Spirit people will worship the Father as he really is, offering him the true worship that he wants. God is Spirit, and only by the Power of his Spirit can people worship him as he really is (Jn 4:23–24).

The motivating power of the Holy Spirit is what is crucial in worship, not the style or the content. The Holy Spirit can move in jingle-style choruses and in the hymns of

Isaac Watts. The Holy Spirit can empower ancient liturgies and children's faltering prayers. He can move through the joy of dance and the solemnity of sung evensong.

People should be given opportunity to worship in ways that are most natural for them. Church leaders should stop trying to make everyone conform to the same patterns of worship and create space for a diversity of styles. In our current situation many worshippers leave church disappointed. As we have struggled to keep everyone together we've actually made the divisions deeper!

There must be frequent opportunities for the local congregation to worship together, but there should also be times for them to worship in separate culture groups. There should be services when old and young worship together, and times when they worship apart; times when 'charismatics' and 'traditionalists' worship as one, and times when they are separate.

It is vital for the congregation to gather together, but there must also be space for individuals to meet with those of like mind. When many different interest groups are allowed to express themselves in the life of a church, its worship life will be all the richer.

A plural community is one in which different groups are free to express their own preferences, rather than adopting one standard 'norm'. Everyone acknowledges that each group has distinctive gifts to offer and that they all share in a rich diversity rather than conforming to the same pattern.

Britain is not one culture—it is many cultures. It is not one people, but many different 'people groups'. British society is not uniform, it is diverse. The church must create space for this rich diversity to be reflected in its worship life. Some of these 'people groups' deserve special mention.

Young people

Taking the Methodist Church as an example, the lack of young people in the church is very disturbing. More than half of Britain's Methodist churches have no members or attenders under the age of 18. Almost half of the membership is aged over 60 and nearly 70% are over 45 years.

Even churches which do have thriving youth fellowships are finding it a struggle to persuade young people to worship regularly. Teenagers would often rather teach in Sunday school than stay in worship. Many young people arrive for their youth group when the evening service is just finishing.

It isn't enough for young people to have an occasional youth service or a favourite chorus in an act of worship. They need space to develop styles of praise which are compatible with their own culture. Youth culture is full of movement, noise, colour, drama, light, life and energy. It's always changing and it has a language and style all its own. Instead of expecting young Christians to conform to 'church culture' we should let them express worship in their own way without being told—'You'll upset Mrs Jones if you do that!'

The Young People's Working Group for the Nationwide Initiative in Evangelism concluded that 'the churches have not provided an atmosphere or a place which can receive the respect of young people and does not cause them to lose face with their peers'.

What has happened is that young people have voted with their feet. Many churches have lost teenagers from regular worship. Young people need space to pray in their own language, sing to their own rhythm, and worship in their own relaxed and unstructured style. But they must also be encouraged to participate in all-age worship and to share their insights with the rest of God's people.

Working-class groups

Many ministers and preachers are unashamedly middle class. Although many come from working class roots their theological training has made them 'middle class'. The way in which church life is structured ensures that most genuine expressions of working class culture are quietly 'dealt with'. Our language, our dress, our behaviour and our ways of thinking often exclude people from working-class backgrounds. The pressure is to become articulate and cultured, and to conform to middle-class 'norms'.

23% of non-churchgoers don't read a newspaper at all. Yet we often ask congregations to use three different books during a one hour service. 19% read the *Daily Mirror*, and 18% read the *Sun*. Very few read the 'quality newspapers' which are so often quoted from our pulpits. We use a kind of language and style which is inaccessible to the person who buys the *Sun*!

According to the annual HMSO statistics publication *Social Trends*, *Coronation Street* has been the most popular television programme. Over a twelve-month period the soap operas were consistently highest in the ratings, with the power to pull over 17 million people to the TV set every week! This demonstrates the level at which most people operate.

The ideas and illustrations which come from our pulpits week by week are a foreign language to many working-class Christians. The style and content does not communicate with the average *Coronation Street* addict.

A friend of mine tried to settle in a large affluent suburban church for over three years, but it didn't work.

Eventually he gave up and joined a small independent church in the centre of a council estate. A few weeks afterwards he phoned me up to say 'I belong!' His faith has blossomed, and his opportunities for ministry have multiplied since moving out of the middle-class church.

People who don't relate to 'concepts' should be offered a style of worship that appeals to 'gut reactions'. People who prefer rhythm to plainsong should be encouraged in their preference. Those who find words a barrier should be allowed to explore feelings instead. There is a rightful place for working-class worship and we must create space for it to develop.

Of course all the social groups must gather together for worship regularly, taking care not to overwhelm those who are less articulate. Clive Calver summed it up when he wrote:

> This is a class-ridden nation, and the Christian faith has become a middle class religion. It is seen in practice as irrelevant to the working man. We need to free our faith from its cultural entrapment.

Ethnic minorities

We live in a society which includes many ethnic minorities. According to the 1981 census about 6% of our population was born outside Britain, a total of nearly 3.5 million people. Many of these have married and had children. Statisticians estimate that about 9% of our population are first or second generation British residents.

Many Christians within the ethnic minorities don't relate to contemporary British worship. Research (Pearson 1978) reveals that it's mainly middle-class black people, or those with middle-class aspirations, who find a home for themselves in the established churches.

The Methodist report *A Tree God Planted* revealed that very few black people have found their way into leadership positions in the local church. Thousands of black Christians have left mainstream churches to join the black-led congregations.

I admire the work of the ministry team of a church in Southall. They arrange for frequent multi-racial services, but they have also encouraged the development of two parallel congregations within their church. On Sunday mornings a predominantly white congregation meets for a traditional free church act of worship. On Sunday afternoons the church is full of Asians for a service in Urdu which relates to their music and culture, and is relevant to the local Asian community.

If more churches had recognized that there is strength in diversity, they would have kept in closer contact with the ethnic minorities. We have expected these groups to accept our traditions instead of giving them space to create worship suited to their own cultures. It's right that the Body gathers together for worship, but there should also be opportunity for times apart!

There is little hope that we are going to win converts from other religions unless things change. It is estimated that in Britain there are 1,500,000 Muslims, 500,000 Hindus, 180,000 Sikhs and 120,000 Buddhists. We may hope that many of them will discover that Jesus Christ is Lord, but are we being realistic when we expect them to accept our religious culture as well? Must they worship Christ with our hymns and our liturgies? I fear that we are making the same mistake as the missionaries in the halcyon days of the Empire; we are dressing up Christianity in Western clothes.

Traditional and experimental groups

As we create space for diversity in worship we mustn't forget those who prefer traditional forms. This important group within the life of the church is in danger of being neglected in these days of change. Profound liturgy, beautiful music, and poetic hymnody must be conserved and passed on for future generations.

Those who favour such expressions are sometimes pushed out, their views are ridiculed and their preferences taken lightly. They are considered 'old fashioned' and 'fuddy duddy' even though their concern is to protect our inheritance for future generations to enjoy. Such people need to meet with the rest of the congregation to share their insights, but they also need opportunities for expressing traditional forms of worship in their own way.

Many Anglican churches have 9 a.m. services with a more traditional feel. There is beautiful music, traditional liturgy and space for quiet meditation. Those who prefer traditional worship are able to enjoy it without restriction, but they are also encouraged to attend Family Services as well.

At the other extreme, there are those who are looking for completely new styles or worship. I met a group in Swindon who worshipped in each other's homes on Sunday evenings. They used records, poems, slides, video, silence and movement to express their praise.

Groups like this should be encouraged to pioneer new styles in worship. Their ideas should be fed back into services when they join the whole congregation for worship.

Charismatic groups

Wherever I go I meet groups of charismatic Christians

who patiently 'endure' worship week by week. Some ministers are afraid of such groups, and hold them tightly within the mainstream worship life of the church. Expressions of charismatic worship are suppressed or even considered an embarrassment.

I long to see charismatic worship given a rightful place in denominational church life. There must be times when the gifts and insights of the charismatics are shared with the whole congregation and when such groups feel part of the 'whole'.

If in recent years those who had entered a charismatic experience had been given every encouragement to meet together for worship, and the free expression of the gifts of the Holy Spirit (the use of tongues, visions, words of knowledge and healing ministries) given full opportunity to develop, many denominational church members would not have left for the freedom of house church worship.

Children

The growth of 'all-age worship' is one of the most significant trends of the last twenty-five years. Churches which were once deeply committed to the Sunday school movement now structure their life around the presence of children in worship.

I think there is much to commend this exciting new trend. If the worship is rich and diverse and shared with parents and families, it can provide the kind of experience which enables children to grow in the knowledge and love of God. It is important that children see adults at prayer and learn how to worship.

It disturbs me, however, that in some churches the work among children has completely disappeared. 'All-age worship' is undoubtedly a good experience for children to have but they also need time and space to praise God in their own energetic way!

Some churches have started midweek clubs where children can hear Bible stories, sing their own songs and pray in ways which are meaningful for them. We can't expect children to grow in Christ if they aren't given the kind of spiritual food that will enable them to develop, and the kind of worship experiences suited to their age and culture. They should sometimes worship apart from the adult congregation.

Give us the vision

For too long we have struggled to present worship as 'unity', and have created 'uniformity'. It's important that people from every part of church life gather together to eat bread and drink wine and proclaim their oneness in the Spirit. It's also important that the church creates sufficient space for different groups of people to enjoy the kind of worship they really find helpful. We need to trust each other to explore the diversity of worship.

The groups exploring these different worship styles needn't be large. Jesus said, 'Where two or three come together in my name, I am there with them' (Mt 18:20). Two or three teenagers with guitars; two or three Asians speaking Urdu; two or three West Indians singing gospel; two or three liturgists using a prayerbook; two or three pioneers exploring creative arts; two or three charismatics using the gifts; two or three children talking to Jesus—two or three worshippers, and HE IS THERE!

Such groups could meet regularly or rarely. They may be small or large. Led by a minister or by someone appointed by the church. It may be on a Sunday, or it could be midweek. It could be in a private house or in a large cathedral. It may go on for years, or serve its purpose after a month or two. It would encourage worshippers to explore their kind of worship without conforming to the strict timetables of 'family services', and to enjoy space for experiment.

Out of this diversity could come a richness and strength which would strengthen the Body of Christ. Out of all these new experiences could flow a stream of new perceptions enriching corporate worship. St Paul summed it up when he wrote: 'Where the Spirit of the Lord is present, there is freedom' (2 Cor 3:17).

Where groups of people gather to enjoy each other's fellowship and to share their own style of worship there is great joy. Such groups act like magnets which draw in others on the fringes of church life who could never relate to 'normal' services. These worship groups are a means of evangelism and a doorway for many into the ongoing life of the church.

Styles of worship are vehicles for our adoration and praise. Some are carried into the presence of the living God by noise and movement. Others are transported by silence and stillness. There is no such thing as first-class and second-class styles of worship. Who are we to judge the relative values of a jingle-chorus or a sixteenth-century hymn? Does the Lord prefer one form of words to another?

It is when the style we are using carries us into the presence of the Lord that we really worship. When we meet him face to face, it doesn't matter whether we got there with the help of pipe organs or electric guitars! We are empowered by the Holy Spirit to worship in spirit and in truth.

A few days ago I was leading a youth service in Huddersfield. The central church was full to overflowing. At the end of the worship we sang the familiar song 'Bind us together'. As we sang and held hands together I sensed that here was a foretaste of the heavenly banquet. In my mind I pictured the great heavenly host bound together by perfect love before the Throne of God.

One day we will not need hymns, choruses, pipe organs, guitars, prayerbooks or liturgies. Worship will be natural and spontaneous. Our greatest experiences of praise here on earth are but a shadow of what we will know. We must prepare ourselves in whatever way we can for the eternal joy of worship which is to come.

After this I looked, and there was an enormous crowd—no one could count all the people! They were from every race, tribe, nation, and language, and they stood in front of the throne and of the Lamb, dressed in white robes and holding palm branches in their hands. They called out in a loud voice: 'Salvation comes from our God, who sits on the throne, and from the Lamb!' All the angels stood round the throne, the elders, and the four living creatures. Then they threw themselves face downwards in front of the throne and worshipped God, saying 'Amen! Praise, glory, wisdom, thanksgiving, honour, power and might belong to our God for ever and ever! Amen!' (Rev 7:9–12).

WORKSHOP SESSION NINE

Starter

Divide into groups of three.

Devise some symbols for different kinds of worship: e.g. a silhouette of a parent pushing a pram for 'family Service', guitars for a 'Youth Service', prayer book for a 'Read Service', etc.

Your church is to be entered in a new *Guide to British Worship*. What symbols would you put beside your church's entry for the different styles of worship it offers?

Are there any missing symbols which you feel should be there?

Share your findings with the whole group.

Discuss: Are there people in your community who would find it hard to relate to worship in your church?

Can anything be done to serve them?

Activity

In groups of three talk about services you have enjoyed—or hated. Recall different styles of worship you've known at Christian festivals, and over past years in your church's worship life. Share experiences of ecumenical services, visits to churches when you've been on holiday, and fellowship meetings you've attended.

List the many different worship experiences mentioned—and put a ✓ by those you found helpful and a ✗ by those you didn't enjoy.

Discuss: Do people like different styles of worship in your church?

Would it be helpful to spend time apart as well as time together?

Discussion questions

1. Jesus said: 'But the time is coming and is already here, when by the power of God's Spirit people will worship the Father as he really is, offering him the true worship that he wants' (Jn 4:23).

What kind of worship do you think God wants?

2. Jesus said: 'God is Spirit, and only by the power of his Spirit can people worship him as he really is' (Jn 4:24).

Do we sometimes worship without the power of the Holy Spirit?

3. Revelation says: 'They were from every race, tribe, nation, and language, and they stood in front of the throne and of the Lamb, dressed in white robes and holding palm branches in their hands' (Rev 7:9).

Has this beautiful vision anything to teach us about how we should worship today?

Closing prayers

Give everyone in the group a large clean sheet of paper.

Each person must imagine that the paper is their local congregation.

Do to the paper what you would like the Lord to do to your local congregation. Each person shares what they've done with the paper. These statements are then turned into prayers. Then pray more generally for the renewal of your church's worship life.

10

Participation and the Arts

In the hot summer of 1981, I toured fifty towns around Britain with a zany comedy presentation called the 'Gospel Roadshow'. We drove from Cornwall to Scotland, and covered every region of the country.

We took with us a gospel rock band, a drama team and a rather decrepit truck called 'Blossom'. During the tour 16,000 young people came to see the presentation, and 3,000 were counselled.

It was an exhausting tour. We travelled every morning, set up the equipment each afternoon and presented 'Gospel Roadshow' each night. After the show there was often a lot of counselling to be done.

Yet everywhere we went, I heard young people saying the same thing! 'We're really into Jesus, but worship is a bore.' From the smallest market towns to affluent suburbia, from inner cities to sprawling council estates, the message came across to us loud and clear.

All over the country young people admitted that they were staying away from services. Even the most enthusiastic and dedicated youth leaders were finding it hard to get their young people to attend worship.

The problem so concerned me that I couldn't sleep. Even weeks after the 'Roadshow' tour had ended I was still deeply disturbed by what I'd seen and heard. I felt that if we were ever to mount another national tour we should try to tackle this need.

It was out of this concern that 'Daybreak' was born. The musical told the story of the Resurrection through the eyes of Mary, Peter and Thomas. Our small production group decided to produce something which would enable young people to celebrate their faith in contemporary style.

The story of 'Daybreak' is a book in itself! What started as the seed of an idea gradually snowballed until the musical was presented in 28 major venues during March 1983 to an audience of 40,000 people. A cast of over 3,000 young people shared in the different performances!

Since then 'Daybreak' has been performed by hundreds of groups all over the British Isles. It has been toured in Australia, Norway, Africa, and Germany. There have also been performances in Russia.

I will never forget the joy of that first 'Daybreak' tour. The commitment which the young people showed was tremendous and their desire to support the event in prayer really impressed me. To them 'Daybreak' was an act of worship. Through this project we realized what gifts the young people had. We came across excellent musicians, dancers and actors who really enjoyed taking part. Teenager after teenager said 'I've never been able to use my gifts for the Lord before.'

Sadly, in many churches participation in worship has become an elitist activity. Most people are rarely encouraged to offer what they have and their gifts are lying dormant.

'Daybreak' also taught me that when young people participate—they learn! Many lives were changed through the 'Daybreak' tour, and some young people are now in the ministry or on the mission field as a result of it. Night after night as we sang 'Lord make me a mountain' we would see members of the cast move forward to commit their lives to the Lord. Many of them had been to church for years, but only fully understood the message when they took part.

I received some very critical letters about the 'Daybreak' production. My team smiled every time the post caught up with us because it always contained some hate-mail addressed to me. These letters were suspicious of using the arts in worship, and some writers accused me of being a heretic! For many critics, worship meant the 'hymn-prayer' sandwich, and anything different was irrelevant, distasteful—and even blasphemous.

In fact, the church's worship tradition in the creative arts is very rich—it's just that many of our critics knew nothing about it! The introduction of music, art, drama and movement into worship wasn't revolutionary at all. It was a rediscovery of our roots.

Tradition

In many areas of the country we have found that dance in worship is frowned upon. We've often been asked to remove the word 'dance' from our publicity as it 'offends people'.

I can understand why. I grew up at a time when dancing was still frowned upon by church members. In some church halls you can still see signs which state 'dancing on these premises is forbidden'. It's little wonder, then, that many people are suspicious of dance in worship! I have to admit that for many years I felt this way about dance in worship, too.

But I have gradually become more and more convinced that dance is a legitimate and important aspect of worship. I have had to re-examine my prejudices and admit that I've been wrong. Dance in worship is nothing new! There are twelve verbs in Biblical Hebrew which mean 'to dance'. They imply circular or ring dances, processional marches, hopping or whirling dances—and the word for Passover also means 'to dance in a limping fashion'.

When the covenant box was taken to Jerusalem with shouts of joy and a fanfare of trumpets, David stopped the procession and 'danced with all his might in honour of the Lord' (2 Sam 6:13–14).

After the Israelites had miraculously crossed the Red Sea there was great rejoicing. Miriam, Aaron's sister, took a timbrel in her hand and led the women in a great dance of celebration! (Ex 15:20).

The news of David's victory over Goliath was sung and danced through Israel. And at least two psalms use words in their titles which imply that they were meant to be accompanied by dance.

Scholars of dance history believe that the early church used dance in its liturgy, and that it was described as a 'heavenly joy'. It seems likely that these dances were absorbed into the early church from Jewish worship.

Dance is nothing new—it's something rediscovered! Sometimes I've watched as a congregation has danced together and there has been an explosion of sheer joy, I have also seen groups minister to congregations in dance and lead the people to the throne of God through it.

Although I am no artist I am totally committed to the use of art in worship. I have seen dark and drab churches light up with a blaze of bright colour. Huge banners, beautiful pictures, modern posters, fascinating three-dimensional shapes and beautiful flower displays can be a genuine expression of worship.

Right from Old Testament times there has been suspicion about art. It's a valid caution and it's based on the second commandment which forbids graven images. I'm sure that at times in church history art and ikons have become 'graven images' and that worshippers have worshipped the created rather than the Creator. But I'm equally convinced that sanctuaries devoid of art do not glorify a God of colour and light in the way that they should.

The early church found novel ways of using art. As a persecuted church they had to put their Christian signs and symbols into pagan Roman art and hide the true Christian meaning.

From the time of Constantine when the church was legalized, art became more prominent. Imperial patronage meant that huge churches could be decorated in magnificent style. Mosaics and marble floors were particularly popular.

By the fifth century, art was being used by Christians for three main purposes; to depict their vision of heaven, to educate others about the Bible and as an inspiration for prayer. Scholars agree that this period was a crucial time in which the church preserved ancient cultural values. When people complain about 'art in the sanctuary' they show that they don't understand the importance of art in church history!

We have a great responsibility to put our faith into visual terms in this visual age, and to make our sanctuaries the place for visually communicating the word. The pictures can be changed every few weeks so that there is always fresh visual interest. Even if a service is 'boring', the church walls can be alive with colourful symbols which will enrich our worship.

Church music can also be a contentious area. I have often heard church organists complaining about the presence of other instruments in worship. Many of them don't realize that the organ was once banned from churches because it was associated with Roman combat!

From the earliest times a wide range of instruments was used in worship. The opening of Solomon's Temple, for example, must have sounded like an orchestral concert!

I would like to see more and more church orchestras involved in contemporary worship. Many people would love to express their praise in music and the church must make provision for this. The growth of church music groups using guitars and keyboards is also a good sign. The greater the diversity of church music used, the broader its appeal will be.

I'm sad that singing in many churches is so staid and unimaginative when our singing tradition is so rich and diverse. Scholars tell us that vocal music was flourishing at the time of Christ and that simple cantorial melodies were absorbed into churches from the synagogues. The heart of Christian song is the sound of many voices slowly singing in unison. This kind of singing dominated Christian worship for a thousand years and is still popular in churches around the world today. It is known as plain-song and is the free melodic chanting of sacred texts. There's a great intensity and serenity about it and it relies on the natural stress of language for its rhythm.

When I was on holiday on the Greek island of Lesbos I visited an ancient monastery and bought a cassette of the choir. They were singing ancient Gregorian chants. I was really moved by this music and astonished to discover that some of our simple modern choruses have a similar sound. Those who think that hymns are 'traditional' may be surprised to discover that the unstructured singing they dislike may stem from an even older tradition!

Worship is really enriched when the whole congregation is involved in creating rhythm, music, harmony and lyric. I long for those who lead church music to launch out and take greater risks! A congregation can suggest phrases to fit a simple tune and then improvise harmonies to enrich it. In doing this they will really get involved in the worship.

Some people feel that drama has no place in worship, but the prophets frequently used dramatic acts to make their point. Jesus told dramatic stories to great effect, and he used humour to communicate to large crowds.

Drama has been part of worship for centuries. It slowly developed as part of the liturgy until it found a place of its own. In the tenth century, Bishop Ethelwold of Winchester's advice to officiating priests sounded like a list of stage directions:

> Let the one still sitting there—as if recalling them—say the anthem 'Come and see the place'. And saying this let him rise, and lift the veil and show them the place bare of the cross, but only the cloths laid there in which the cross was wrapped.

Slowly the liturgy began to include 'trope'—new illustrative material alongside the main text. Free drama evolved from this, and soon whole episodes or 'cycles' appeared. These 'cycle plays' gradually grew in popularity. They usually told the story of man from creation to the Last Judgement. Each cycle was composed of between twenty-five and fifty short plays, all of which were presented in a major religious centre such as a cathedral city.

These cycles were major events. They involved the whole community and large numbers of clergy. The drama was performed in churches or market squares and it communicated Bible stories. Organizers hoped that by participating in the drama the local people would be strengthened in their faith.

Drama in worship is nothing 'new' or 'revolutionary'. It's theatre returning to its roots in the liturgy. In drama, as with all the arts, Christians should inject creativity into worship and out into the wider culture in which they live.

Beginnings

Following 'Daybreak' I became committed to the renewal of worship through the participative arts. We toured our 'Travelling Workshop' training day to fifty-five towns in 1984 and 1985. Then came 'Tell It With Joy', full weekends of workshops and celebration in over sixty towns during 1986 and 1987.

We discovered that workshops worked best when people of a wide age-range were involved. When only teenagers were taking part people said 'Oh no, not another youth service', and stayed away. Others sat in the congregation and treated the whole thing like a performance. They made patronizing comments like 'Didn't they do well', which really irritated the young people.

When we used groups of ages eleven to eighty years we found the workshops took on a much greater credibility. Ministers and lay folk learnt how to move, eighty-year olds and young marrieds worked on art, teens and senior citizens improvised drama together. There was an inherent power when material was presented by such a wide age-range. Even the most sceptical members of the congregation sat up and took notice of the worship!

We also had to learn that 'experts' weren't welcome. When participants showed an attitude of 'superiority' toward others in the workshop, it was doomed. Those who had no experience felt threatened and unworthy, and those who thought of themselves as 'experts' begrudged working with beginners.

We insisted that everyone came in an attitude of humility and with an eagerness to learn. No group would be dominated by an 'expert' elite. Sometimes we encouraged trained singers to try art, or good artists to attempt creative writing, so that they could experience something new.

We were also at great pains to point out that everyone had something to offer. We discovered people who had been told they couldn't sing but who had good voices, and those who thought they were hopeless at art but who were able to produce beautiful work.

Each group had no 'experts' and no 'failures', and was primed to become a creative nucleus. Individuals supported and encouraged each other. We stamped out any hint of competition in the workshops and reminded people that they were about pleasing God, not 'playing to the gallery'.

We also discovered that workshop leaders needed to be 'enablers' rather than 'teachers'. Those who had the best artistic qualifications didn't necessarily make the best workshop leaders! Some leaders with no qualifications at all could really motivate a group into creative activity.

Workshop leaders were encouraged to approach each group with a desire to learn rather than teach. They spent time putting every member of the group at ease and enabling them to get enthusiastic about the media they were working in.

Workshop leaders also realized that their task was a spiritual one. There was no division between the 'workshop' and the 'worship celebration'. Groups moved from activity to prayer and back again without interruption. There was a sense of ministry throughout the workshop, and a special awareness of the presence of the Lord.

Exploration of worship is something which should continually evolve. Choirs which have met for years on end can become stale and bored and their music ministry become a 'duty' rather than a 'joy'. Creative art workshops should be disbanded, if they ever deteriorate in the same way. The groups should not become too stable or their meetings become too much of a ritual. If they do get stale they should move on to explore a new medium or to involve new members in the group.

Creativity brings joy, colour and life to the drabbest services. It brings an excitement which is caught by others in the congregation and creates a new dynamic which encourages everyone to share what they can.

All this has enormous consequences for the ordering of church life. Responsibility for worship will be shifted from preachers to 'worship groups.' Those who lead the church's music will need to learn a greater flexibility. Pews will need to be pulled out and flexible spaces created for dance and drama. Money, personnel and plant will need to be allocated by church headquarters so that workshop leaders can be trained. Many of us will have to take new risks as we allow others to share in worship and 'do their thing.'

I long to see worship which is alive!–unpredictable!–joyful!–colourful!–meaningful!–special! I long to see it every week! I believe it's possible, and I see the seeds of it in many parts of the country. Worship should be the highlight of the week and we must invest time and energy to ensure that it is so. Creative worship honours our Creator God. It is the bringing of the best we have to offer. And no one can ever say it's boring . . .

WORSHIP WORKSHOPS

At the conclusion of the course gather the group together for one or more 'Worship Workshops'. Invite others from the church to join. Ask people with special skills to come as 'enablers'.

Arrange with the minister or church leaders for your work to be included in the following Sunday's worship. Each workshop should last about two and a half hours. Get the theme of the service from the minister beforehand, and produce material which will be appropriate.

The workshop could be held on a midweek evening or on a Sunday afternoon in preparation for an evening service. If appropriate, all the workshops could be run simultaneously and then fed into one celebration. If the people don't know each other well, precede each workshop with ten minutes of informal sharing.

1. Drama (5–10 participants)

(The basic format of this workshop can also be used for a Dance/Movement workshop).

Equipment needed:Bibles, interesting props to get people's imagination going, costumes, books of drama games.

30 mins a. Without introduction, the group plays confidence-building drama games. (From drama books in most libraries.)

20 mins b. Pray for one another. Read the 'theme' passage (simple Bible stories make the best 'theme' passages). Talk about the 'theme' and pray together.

15 mins c. Divide into threes and script, improvise or role-play one section of the 'theme' passage.

20 mins d. Watch each 'three' present what they have

created. After each presentation, ask the whole group to add suggestions as to how it could be developed.

10 mins e. Move back into groups of three for more detailed scripting and improvisation, so that each section is a lot tighter. Move back together as a whole group.

15 mins f. Appoint a director from within the group to tighten and direct the whole piece. The director merges the different sections into one, involving everyone in the group.

15 mins g. Encourage people to improvise their parts, and give encouragement.

25 mins h. Move to where the drama will be presented and work on volume, entrances, exits, props, and costume. Rehearse the piece three times.

Total time: approximately 2 hours 30 minutes.

2. Art (15–20 participants)

Equipment needed:*For banners*: Long roll of heavy neutral coloured cloth, lots of remnants, strong glue, brushes, scissors, needles and thread.

For art: Rolls of paper and art-paper, brushes, children's powder paint, felt-tip pens, pencils and rubbers.

For flowers: A wide range of flowers, greenery and stands, rocks, and wood for building interesting shapes; scissors and thread.

Ladders, string, blue-tack and tape for putting together the displays.

20 mins a. Get people drawing and painting as quickly as possible and establish a positive and creative atmosphere.

20 mins b. Pray for one another. Move into study of the 'theme section' from the Bible.

30 mins c. In the sanctuary, talk about what you'd like to create.

15 mins d. Work together in 'threes' on ideas, signs, symbols and pictures which communicate the theme.

5 mins e. Everyone shares their signs, symbols and pictures. Discuss ideas about the end results.

5 mins f. Divide into media groups. i.e. flowers, banners and art. Each group moves into the sanctuary to discuss what they will make and how it will be displayed.

60 mins g. Work in media groups to create the end result. Each person is involved in the group. Work should be quick and simple!

10 mins h. Display the work in suitable areas around the sanctuary.

Total time: approximately 2 hours 30 minutes.

3. Music (20–30 participants)

Equipment needed: Manuscript paper, Bibles, hymn books, biros, paper, piano, large roll of paper, felt tips, duplicator + typewriter or overhead projector, musical instruments, music edition of song books.

20 mins a. Get the group singing. Start with material they are familiar with, then move on quickly to simple new material. It should be easy to

harmonize and sing with a strong rhythm.

20 mins b. Study the Bible 'theme' section, and discuss together. Pray for one another.

10 mins c. As a group discuss what kind of hymn or song you think would best communicate the 'theme' passage. Choose a hymn to model yours on.

60 mins d. Divide into two groups. Five people are to compose the tune. They should be musicians, and at least one should be able to score music.

The rest compose the lyrics. They subdivide into groups of four for this task. Allocate each group a section of the Bible 'theme' to work on.

10 mins e. The musicians return and teach the new music to the others. Don't proceed until everyone knows the tune well! Meanwhile the lyrics are written on a large roll of paper.

10 mins f. The groups sing through the lyrics to the new tune, making amendments until the words 'fit' the tune.

The words on the roll of paper are corrected accordingly.

10 mins g. The musicians present rehearse the hymn while the choir work on rhythm, pace and harmony.

10 mins h. Rehearse the finished hymn in the sanctuary and practice entrances and exits.

i. The words are duplicated for the congregation. The choir sings the hymn once through before the congregation joins in.

Total time: approximately 2 hours 30 minutes.

4. Creative writing (5 participants)

Equipment needed:Biros, paper, 'trigger' pictures from newspapers or brochures. Samples of interesting writing.

20 mins a. The group brings favourite books and written articles, and these are shared. They can be on any subject and should illustrate a variety of styles.

20 mins b. Study the Bible 'theme' section and discuss together. Pray for one another.

10 mins c. Discuss what kind of written media you'd like to use; e.g. storytelling, meditation, rhyming poetry, free verse, testimony, letters, dialogue, prayers, phrases, speeches, etc.

60 mins d. Work individually or in pairs on your chosen subject-matter and style format. It may be helpful to move right away from the rest of the group. Return with finished work.

30 mins e. Share your work together and choose the sections which you feel are most appropriate for the celebration. Those whose pieces are not chosen are invited to read the selected pieces, so that everyone's involved!

10 mins f. Move into the sanctuary and rehearse the readings—check for volume, diction and presentation.

Total time: Approximately 2 hours 30 minutes.